DAVID BOOTH

Story Drama

Creating stories through role playing, improvising, and reading aloud
2nd Edition

Pembroke Publishers Limited

For Kathy and Chuck Lundy

© **2005 Pembroke Publishers**
538 Hood Road
Markham, Ontario, Canada L3R 3K9
www.pembrokepublishers.com

Distributed in the U.S. by Stenhouse Publishers
480 Congress Street
Portland, ME 04101-3400
www.stenhouse.com

We acknowledge the financial support of the Government of Canada through the Book Publishing Industry Development Program (BPIDP) for our publishing activities.

We acknowledge the support of the Government of Ontario through the Ontario Media Development Corporation Book Fund.

Library and Archives Canada Cataloguing in Publication

Booth, David
    Story drama : creating stories through role playing, improvising, and reading aloud / David Booth. — 2nd ed.

Includes bibliographical references and index.
ISBN 1-55138-192-3

    1. Drama in education. 2. Language arts—Correlation with content subjects. 3. Language arts (Elementary) I. Title.

PN3171.B66 2005   372.139'9   C2005-903729-6

Editor: Kate Revington
Cover Design: John Zehethofer
Typesetting: Jay Tee Graphics Ltd.

Printed and bound in Canada
9 8 7 6 5 4 3 2 1

Contents

Introduction: Students and Teachers Learning through Drama

I remember the first time I tried whole-group drama—a departure from the constant instructions and contrived skits that characterized my teaching before I better understood the nature of drama. It was with a Grade 8 gifted class at Dalewood Public School in Hamilton. I had just returned from a workshop at Queen's University with educator Brian Way, and I thought, *I'm going to try this no matter what*. I put on some music, the class moved the desks to the sides of the room, I told the students to find places by themselves, and I said: "You are underwater and you're going to find treasure. You are moving in slow motion as you swim near the wrecks of previous centuries." And what those students did non-verbally with their bodies thrilled me to my core. I suddenly recognized the power of letting the drama emerge from the students' imaginations, and I have never looked back.

Finding Treasure

On early practice: If only I had understood the nature of drama and had also moved into improvised language, my life would have been so much easier. In truth, there were few plays written for students at this age, and students need so much experience understanding themselves and their own lives that role playing could have been the answer all along.

This book is a record of the almost 40 years I have spent working in story drama, with my classroom drama classes and students loaned to me by co-operative teachers as demonstration classes, while groups of teachers and student teachers both observed and, most important, participated in the experience. When I use the term *students* in my writing, the participants could be from 5 to 50 years of age. In drama, *everyone* is a student, and everyone teaches. Working in such a context provided me with opportunities to explore alongside new teachers and teachers new to drama from inside the learning, as we visited schools, brought students to our drama studio, or worked in drama demonstrations at conferences.

I find it difficult to believe that so many years have passed, but as I reread my notes, the students' faces pop into view with each transcript, captured in drama moments. When triggered, I can recall faces and incidents from every group of students with whom I have worked, moments of drama that have seeped into my unconscious and that reappear, seemingly from nowhere, during subsequent teaching encounters. As well, I have had the good fortune to spend hours with teachers after the students had left, discussing the ideas explored, the students' words and phrases, the teachers' responses to the role playing, the questions that remained unanswered, the strategies that awaited implementation with the next group.

"The Singer, the Song, the Sung"

I found Caldwell Cook's *The Play Way* (1917) an amazing record of a teacher's work with story and drama. His book was the earliest to propose the use of drama in this way. Cook believed that children learn better from doing and experiencing than from just reading and listening.

In my work, story and drama are forever linked. Even now, when I am reviewing a new picture book or novel for children, I cannot escape the possibilities that flood my drama-structured mind. Similarly, when preparing to work with a group of youngsters for the first time in drama, I cannot imagine entering the room without a range of stories ready to tell or read aloud. Perhaps I require the safety net of narrative in order to attempt the leap into creating stories together through drama. Or have I become a "storyer," linking incidents and events that the students and I experience together into a narrative that echoes the books and tales that have gone before, trying to connect the students and myself to the story network that gives meaning to our lives?

Over the years, I have seen a single tale give rise to a hundred different treatments and interpretations, determined by the participants and the moment, each story drama unique, yet caught somewhere within the original story's fabric. *Story drama*—which I'll define, for the moment, as improvised role play stimulated by a story—surrounds my teaching. It allows students to at once become the co-constructors of a story, the story itself, and the characters living within the story: as the poet David McCord says, they are "the singer, the song and the sung."

Teachers need to teach, and students need to be taught by teachers who somehow reflect on what has gone on, so that their future work can be informed and illuminated by past experience. I would hope the stories we tell one another about working with students would cause us to change as teachers. As teachers, we need wise mentors to point the way and guide our reflections, but more than that, we need others who continue to find joy and satisfaction in the struggle to teach, who extend and enrich us with their own explorations, working together with students inside the art form, holding the paint brush, talking in role, singing the song, dancing the dance. We must always find a way of entering the arts experience.

Any teacher can use story drama to teach, even if it is a rough, improvised session that lasts only a few minutes. Over the years, I have noticed a range of styles among teachers of drama: from energetic young apprentices who become the whole drama, leaving students to stare in wonder, to thoughtful practitioners who draw from these young role players concentrated and focused affective thought. Whatever the style or situation, however, story drama can have powerful results.

Teachers often tell me that they can't replicate my results in the classroom, though. After all, as a guest teacher, I appear for a few hours or days, armed with plans and stories that I have prepared well in advance, and without all the other responsibilities classroom teachers have. "What will the students be like when your novelty wears off?" I am asked. "You have the time to prepare for one two-hour lesson; we have to keep teaching." And, most often, because I ask the adults observing to work in role whenever possible, I hear, "We don't have a bunch of teaching volunteers in our classrooms."

These are, of course, valid points, but expecting a teacher to replicate a story drama lesson is *never* the intent. A visiting teacher's session can suggest new ideas and approaches, as can any guest's involvement with the

I owe my drama training to two great leaders in educational drama in England: Dorothy Heathcote and Gavin Bolton. The books listed below discuss their approaches.

Dorothy Heathcote: Drama as a Learning Medium, Revised edition, by Betty Jane Wagner

Acting in Classroom Drama by Gavin Bolton

students, or an excursion to a gallery, a theatre performance, a trip to the classroom across the hall, or a celebration on parents' night. Students learn all the time in different ways, and a demonstration lesson allows the classroom teacher to observe the students in a different context. In every instance, teachers comment that they have learned something new about one or more of their students.

At times, the classroom teacher is nervous in a public setting with a guest teacher, focused on wanting the students to do well and to feel valued. I remember my first years of teaching, when Bill Moore, my language arts supervisor in Hamilton, would ask if he could work with my class. I would retreat to the back of the room, still controlling each student with invisible threads to be manipulated by me in secret. When I eventually let loose those ties and relaxed as Bill set free the students into new patterns of behavior, new status roles, and new dynamics of interaction, only then did those students emerge into fully rounded human beings for me—it was a bit like watching a Polaroid picture developing over time. On each occasion when Bill Moore visited, I learned more about teaching and more about my students, and more about what I wanted to become.

When I work with students and teachers, I quickly lose myself in the medium of classroom drama, but the students are front and centre in the learning. Over the years, noted educator Dorothy Heathcote taught me to ensure that those watching not respond as an audience being entertained, but as participants engaged in the struggle to understand the teaching/learning dynamic.

Reflecting for the Journey

Because of the format of demonstration teaching, where we work as a whole group, in small groups, with partners, and independently, teacher-participants can begin to develop their subsequent contributions from the feedback the students give when drawn together from time to time. The strengths and abilities that teachers possess never cease to amaze me, and I watch both them and the students, taking direction for the work from the hesitant, yet productive, interactions. A young teacher once complained to me that during discussions in role, I was not calling upon her for suggestions, and when I explained that my focus was on the students' work, she replied that she, too, had ideas to contribute.

Certainly, the dual roles of participant and observer can be frustrating for teachers working inside the drama and alongside the students; however, moments of learning can grow from that tension. During reflection, first with the students, and then with the adults, the opportunities for drama growth multiply. When the community listens to its members revealing and commenting upon their experiences, members can benefit from the variety of observations being offered, selecting those reflections that will illuminate their own journeys. As well, students often write to me about our visits, and a new set of observations appears for further consideration. Teachers, too, bring back their thoughts in journals and papers, distanced from the moment, and placed in context within their own teaching lives. Some of the insightful comments included in this book provide evidence of this.

On dynamic teaching: By reflecting on their own teaching, by talking with experts in the field and colleagues, and by reading articles and books about drama education, teachers learn what it is to be a changing teacher, to continue to reach each year's students in new and better ways.

During the years, as teachers pondered our demonstrations, together in class and alone in their journals, I recognized that their collective reflections reveal all of the concerns we have in drama in education today. If we would listen to those educators working with students, and if we could become part of the negotiated meaning-making that grows from these interactions, then the teaching/learning process in drama could be revealed and clarified from within the truth of the classroom. The comments by the teachers in this book are drawn from their journals, their group interactions, and their post-course reflections. Their voices represent the variety of responses that emerged from teachers as they brought their own experiences to both participatory classroom demonstrations and seminars. Many teachers had worked with or read every drama authority in contemporary education; some of them were actors and storytellers, graduates of theatre arts programs; some were new to drama teaching, but brought finely honed curriculum-connected strengths.

My personal reflections in this book are often interspersed with comments from teacher-participants that I think can deepen us as a teaching/learning community. I have left these comments anonymous because usually the thoughts of many have been caught by one voice. I have also transcribed the voices of students, and have included examples of their reflections and thoughts about drama experiences in letters received from them, after they returned to their classrooms and their own school programs. These letters often reveal a moment in the drama I had missed or misjudged, or demonstrate further insight by the students from the cool distance of "after the events." I treasure them, and each time I read through a bundle that a teacher has been kind enough to send me, I am struck again by the clarifying that occurs when we consider the implications of what we have taken part in.

Strategies for Supporting Story Drama

The following list distills some ideas that teachers of drama can apply when working with students in their classrooms. The chapters that follow reinforce and expand on many of these suggestions.

- Find authentic reasons for viewing the work of different groups. The drama work will grow stronger for the whole class because of what is learned in the group sharing. Invite students to watch a group present its work with the intent of gaining a collective understanding to be used in developing the drama further. We can use what we have observed to build a stronger context for the drama work.
- "Paste" the separate work of different groups into an ensemble presentation to create an integrated whole.
- Be sure to pause improvisational work in order to refocus the energy and the direction of the students. You can use still images of aspects of the drama, or narrate what has happened thus far in the building of the theme.
- Build your drama events around the whole class, never a favored few. Be certain individual and group work leads to the whole-class creation. As the drama progresses, help students to find research on the Internet, and in newspapers and books. It can add to the quality of the drama being constructed.
- When the class or groups become unfocused or unmanageable, stop the drama, come together, and find ways to move forward without resorting to complaining.
- If the drama is wandering or lacks direction, stop it, and with the students, edit and revise the work, feeling free to cut scenes that no longer add to the work's main theme.
- Choose structures, techniques, and conventions that suit the theme of the drama exploration and that add to the understanding of what is being represented.
- Continue to browse through picture books, songs, novels, poems, songs, newspapers, history texts, and art books for ideas for drama.
- Use recorded music to create mood and atmosphere in the drama work; narrate a story that summarizes the drama that has been created.
- Move the drama ahead in time and space: what happens when …, it is ten years since….
- As the drama unfolds in the "present moment," flashback scenes can be inserted to explain the past incidents that have an impact on what is happening. These prior experiences can give meaning to a complex character or help the students understand the reasons for the present situation.
- Use still pictures to explore the theme, to focus on details, to compare events, to clarify an issue.
- Have the students sometimes work in silence, using movement, mime, and dance as part of the content of the drama you are exploring together.
- Create a contextual frame around the drama in order to build the work towards a cohesive whole. Determine with the students the theme, the time, and the place.
- Start the improvisation again: change roles; alter the positions of the role players; change the perspective. You might watch a scene again to review what happened in more detail or to determine the truth being represented.

- Play several scenes at one time to gain an overall impression of the theme being explored, or the mood being created.
- Be sure to re-energize yourself by attending workshops and seminars, and by having professional discussions about drama with colleagues and student teachers.
- Read texts written by drama educators to see how they work in drama, and add the strategies they discuss to your own repertoire.
- In-role interviews offer students opportunities to question members in order to elicit information, motives, or attitudes. There may be several students working in role as interviewers, and the interviewee may require support from advisers, coaches, or the teacher in role. What is discovered in the interview can be then incorporated into the drama. Interrogations are a formalized version of interviews and can add great tension to work.
- *Hot-seating* is an interview strategy that can be used with an individual or a group working in role. The character(s) on the hot seat is questioned by others in the class. These students may be in role trying to clarify a situation or to glean more information about the hot-seated character(s).
- Types of formal gatherings allow the whole class to participate as an ensemble at events such as meetings, assemblies, inquiries, and protests. The chair or the one in charge is responsible for controlling the proceedings, helping the audience negotiate among speakers, and ensuring that alternatives are presented. Often, group work can be brought to a whole-class setting using this strategy.
- Students in role can make reports about conversations they have overheard or imagined speakers in the drama making. They might also report rumors or gossip, all with the end of adding tension and providing background for the drama.
- By intercutting two or more scenes that depict an event in the drama, the students can focus on the links, contradictions, or ironies that connect seemingly different scenes at different times or in difference places. New meanings can be made through this juxtaposition of sides of an issue or of different times in the life of a character.

Chapter 1: Building a Storying Community

Storying is the process of narrative telling. In trying to find "essential meanings in life," we objectify our experiences by translating them into narrative, which we may then play out in our mind and which we may also communicate to others.

Bill Manson

In story drama, there is the story we begin with—our *shared* story; the story of the drama—our *created* story; and the stories triggered by the drama from students' life experiences—our own *life* stories. As teachers, we work with students as co-constructors of a common story, represented through drama, based on and integrating pieces of the stories we have met and the stories we have lived. As a community, we build another story together through improvisation, always experimenting, slowly putting each piece of our work together until we have our story told and shown "in action." *Story drama* is a process whereby those involved create a new story that all of us own.

Drama allows us to tell stories, to engage in the art of narrative. The simplest retelling of yesterday's events is an act of imagination, as we have the option of reinventing the characters, experiences, circumstances, motivations, and outcomes. Fictional storytelling, like drama, encompasses and extends the possibilities of human experience. Perhaps higher level thought could be called "brain fiction," as Harold Rosen put it, built up by the narrative mind. Drama may be one of the few language situations in school that opens up story possibilities, that allows spontaneous narrative to enter naturally into the flow of talk—every kind of story from personal experience to literary fictions—so that the narrative mode can be an integral part of the school curriculum.

When students try to make meaning with the stories of others, they go back and forth between the story they are reading or listening to and the stories they know, their own personal narratives. They are, in a real sense, building a personal story from the other fictional story, attempting to make sense of the story in order to make more meaning in their lives—until students can make their own stories from the fictional one, there is no story growth for them. The process of *storying*, that is, participating in the sharing, interpreting, representing, and creating of a story, continues beyond the end of the lesson, as the seed of another story readies itself for germination. Sociologist Fred Inglis calls culture "the collection of stories we tell to ourselves about ourselves." Story drama lets us participate in this cultural process of story making together.

Discovering the Heart of Story

Drama is the act of crossing into the world of story. In sharing drama, we agree to live as if the story we are constructing is true. We imagine being

Beginning in 1920, Winifred Ward, at Northwestern University, developed a theory of story dramatization, in which a group of children make a story come alive by playing it out informally, without elaborate scripts or sets. Some drama authorities attacked the limitations of story dramatization, though. They claimed that the goals of enactment are unclear; that the students may imitate, rather than experience dramatic moments; that the desire to sequence story events correctly may lessen the understanding of the greater meanings in the story; and that improvisational work may descend to repeating trivial details in an attempt to re-create the right "facts." These concerns are important for the teacher of drama, but may be a result of not understanding what the story's value is in its relationship to drama.

Into the Story: Language in Action through Drama, by Juliana Saxton and Carole S. Miller, provides carefully worked out scenarios for building effective story dramas.

in the story world. We engage with it, struggle with its unfamiliar concepts, associate our own experience with it, and fill in its shape with our particular interpretation. We process the key events, images, and themes of story by living them out in drama. The process holds true whether the stimulus for the drama is a written story, an oral tale, or an incident from life. Drama enables us to discover the heart of story through the ideas and images we take from it. The voice of the group resonates off the voice of the text to create the voice of the drama.

Using the ideas of a story as cues for their own dramatic responses allows students to test the implications of the text and of their own responses to it. As teacher, I can draw upon the vast resources of the story as a way of stimulating and enriching the students' search for meaning in drama. Groups can test and clarify the implications of the text collectively, so that each person can see the difference in the various perceptions and interpretations, then determine his or her own responses.

We need to provide structure for "now" time. In teaching students to read, we develop structures to help them work inside the print mode as they experience the words; similarly, when working with students in drama, we seek ways of promoting learning as the drama is happening, not just afterwards.

In drama and in narrative, the context may be fictional, but the emotional responses are real. Although the student is in a make-believe situation in story and in drama, the real world still exists, and the learning for the student lies in the negotiation of meanings—symbolic and literal—taking place in both spheres. Drama helps students wander in the story garden, reconstructing symbols, images, and narrative sequences through action. Students re-examine the story's ideas, experimenting with them, learning to "play" with the narrative and then, in reflection, coming to an understanding of both the story's possibilities and the art form used to create new stories.

Drama can help students see beyond literal meaning, even subconsciously, so that an understanding of the complexity and subtlety of meaning may be applied to *every* story explored. The students pause in a fictional present, linger on an image, move forward, backwards, and sideways, all in an attempt to make meaning. Time can be altered, ideas juxtaposed. If story is being used as the source of a drama, then the student brings to the text abilities to hypothesize, to identify with and clarify what is happening in the story, in the drama, and in his or her own life. The learning is integrated as the student engages with the two art forms: the story and the drama. When the student has translated a selection into experience, that student can then re-examine the story in the light of this new experience. Drama lets us take a journey, as Tolkien says, "there and back again."

Making sense of a story demands that the students apply their own experiences to those explored in the story. The teacher's role is to constantly help the students go back and forth between the story and their own responses to it, letting them translate the experiences of the story into the context of their own lives. Drama, then, allows the students' own subjective world to come into play. It helps students explore the intricate meanings of the story as they live through the creating of other, connected stories in drama.

Recognizing universal themes

Many questions and concerns arise when we consider how to approach story drama. If narrative and drama give form to thought and feeling, can we make use of one to build the other? Are they two sides of one coin? Do I risk diminishing one if I include the other at the same time in my teaching? Can we use drama to clarify and strengthen the reading of story, and can we use the story to stimulate or enlighten the drama work? Is it possible for the students to be involved in learning both through drama and through reading in the same frame of reference? How will we engage students in the lifeblood of the story? How will they go about these tasks? Will they improvise within the story, stand on the story's shoulders, or build on the story by designing new contexts or by finding analogies and patterns? How will they place it alongside others, building a set of stories for future reference?

Instead of planning in a vacuum, I can begin with a story that I know well and find the power of drama within it. I can draw on the resources of the story—its situations, characters, problems, relationships, mood, atmosphere, texture and, especially, its concepts—as a way of stimulating and enriching the students' exploration in drama. Both story and drama demonstrate a concern for people—their values, their beliefs, the experiences they live through.

Educator Gavin Bolton says that before planning the drama, the teacher must consider the story from its broadest themes; he says, too, that the goal of all questions is to prod the students' thinking towards universal themes and concepts. The effective teacher searches for a possible starting point that is relevant to the students' experience and relevant to the spirit of the story. Replaying the story through a literal enactment of the plot may have occasional value, but the teacher should not feel limited to it. Typically, the response in these sorts of enactments does not go beyond memory or recapitulation.

Story drama frees the teacher and students from the pressure of acting out the whole story or remembering a script. Most important, the students are allowed to bring what they know to the drama: the drama then engages their imaginations, and they inevitably move closer to the story. We create our own stories through drama, collective stories that may resemble the story or stories we began with (those we have read, heard or seen), draw upon similar contexts or characters, or be based on themes and issues found in the story; or, the drama may explore the story at one remove through an analogy that unlocks internal comprehension. Because of the brain's ability to use metaphor, it can use the pattern of one set of images to organize quite a different set. Story drama, then, can open the door to an endless number of linkages in the story-making events in our lives.

Demonstration: Crowns of Ice—Thinking Creatively

We sometimes forget that students role-play naturally from the time they can first move about: drama is the very stuff of their casual play—imagining an old crate as a castle, a stool as a horse, a paintbrush as a magic wand.

As if there were a basic difference between the fairy tale that a child made up himself and one that was created for him by imaginative folk or by a good writer! ... It makes no difference whether or not the child is offered fairy tales for, if he is not, he becomes his own Andersen, Grimm, Ershov. Moreover, all his playing is a dramatization of a fairy tale which he creates on the spot, animating, according to his fancy, all objects, converting any stool into a train, into a house, into an airplane, or into a camel.

Korneil Chukofsky, *From Two to Five*

John Burningham's picture book *Would You Rather . . .* shows how natural this play is, and provides a perfect vehicle for blending story and drama when working with students. It also provides a useful working model for an examination of the relationship between these two modes of learning. From the very first page, readers are inside the book, as the author invites them to make a choice from among three situations:

> Would you rather
> Your house was surrounded by
> water, snow or jungle.

John Burningham's gentle books can ease us into thinking in an "as if" world, and lead into role work.

Would You Rather . . .
Come Away from the Water, Shirley
The Shopping Basket

Immediately, the students can begin choosing the environment that conjures up for them the most vivid images. When I add, "You are living in your house in that place at this very moment. Tell me what it is like," the element of dramatic involvement is introduced; the students spontaneously become a part of the literary fiction, identifying with their own particular vision of life "there and then" while working "here and now." Authors use this magic "as if" to draw the reader inside the life of a story, and drama works on the same premise. Students who have had experience in creating their own dramatized stories may bring a greater sense of expectation to print: the speculative nature of spontaneous role playing develops the ability to think creatively, to examine the many levels of meaning that underlie each action, and to develop the "what if" element necessary for reading. Just as a story can affect the drama to follow, the learning experience in drama can increase the student's storehouse of personal meanings, thus increasing any meaning he or she brings to the text.

Be sure to check out this resource: *A Child's Work: The Importance of Fantasy Play* by Vivian Gussin Paley.

Involving students through questions

Because of the nature of my work, I generally meet a class of students once in a demonstration setting; therefore, I choose books that generate an immediate response to move them into a situation where we can begin building the "as if" world of drama. *Would You Rather . . .* opens doors at once with students of every grade level. As I read and show the book, I stop every so often to let the students contribute their responses and feelings about the author's ideas through storytelling and dramatic role playing. By questioning students as if they are in role, I can help them picture that world, and the role gives them the public voice with which to share the creations of their imaginations.

GRADE 1 STUDENT: My house is surrounded by water.
DB: *Do you live on an island, or perhaps a houseboat?*
STUDENT: A peninsula, but you can't get to the top end. It's landlocked by a mountain.
DB: *Do you have a boat?*
STUDENT: Not a motor boat. No one in my family believes in them. We only use sailboats.
DB: *Well, what do you do if there is an emergency and no wind?*
STUDENT: There is a kayak, and I can paddle it very fast and go for help. There is a boat ambulance on the mainland.

As I interact with the students, using their own ideas, I can help them begin to understand the consequences of what they are seeing and saying, and together we fashion their own imaginings into a personal, coherent story. Dramatic role playing helps the students go one step beyond identifying and empathizing with the story; they begin to use the story elements to structure their own thoughts, reacting and responding personally, entering as deeply as they wish into the new world of meaning. Through drama, students may move from the particular experience of the story to a more general understanding of what is being explored, making explicit much of what is implied.

> Would you rather be made to eat
> spider stew, slug dumplings, mashed worms,
> or drink snail pop.

GRADE 5 STUDENT: Snail pop.

DB: *Where did you get it?*

STUDENT: Me and my dad make it every summer. First, you catch the snails. We invented these neat traps. Then you begin the process of turning them into the drink.

DB: *How do you go about that?*

STUDENT: Well, it's all based on distillation. The important thing is that you just use the essence of snail, none of the meat.

DB: *Why?*

STUDENT: It clogs the straws when you drink the pop.

DB: *And what do you put the pop in?*

STUDENT: Cans.

DB: *Why not bottles?*

STUDENT: Well, my dad and me used bottles once, but there was a problem. The night we did it, my dad woke me up at midnight, and he said that they were exploding all over the place because we had used too much yeast, and so we had to take all of the bottles into the backyard and bury them, so that no one would be hurt.

As this student built his personal story spontaneously in role by storytelling, he used his own knowledge and background to elaborate upon the literary stimulus.

Promoting lateral thinking

Drama tells me what a student has taken from a story, so that I can help that student examine and explore the possibilities of what has been read, heard, or viewed. Through such externalized representations as drama, students' perceptions are altered and expanded. As students grow in dramatic ability, they improve their communication skills, grappling with experiences, playing out problems, and learning to use the conventions of the medium.

> Would you rather . . .
> An elephant drank your bathwater
> An eagle stole your dinner

A pig tried on your clothes
or a hippo slept in your bed?

These delightful choices can promote much lateral thinking among the students, as they hitchhike on each other's stories, elaborating, extending, and inventing scenarios that help them make sense of the ridiculous, building networks of meaning from each imaginative situation.

As a Grade 2/3 class and I explored the events in *Would You Rather . . .*, the following dialogues occurred.

STUDENT 1: An elephant stole my bathwater.

DB: *Were you in the bath at the time?*

STUDENT 1: Yes.

DB: *Do you mean the elephant drank the dirty bathwater?*

STUDENT 1: No! Elephants just put the water up their trunk so that they can use it later on.

DB: *Was the elephant a pet, was it from the circus, or was it a wild one?*

STUDENT 1: It was the neighbor's.

STUDENT 2: An eagle stole my dinner.

DB: *What were you having for dinner?*

STUDENT 2: Every vegetable you can think of.

DB: *A pig tried on your clothes?*

STUDENT 3: Yes, my jeans, my T-shirt, my socks, and my Adidas.

DB: *Why do you think it did that?*

STUDENT 3: It wanted to see me naked.

DB: *A hippo slept in your bed? Did it break it?*

STUDENT 4: Yes, but it didn't mean to.

DB: *What did your mother say?*

STUDENT 4: Well, I was afraid to tell the truth, because I had been warned about having all of these zoo creatures in my room, and my parents had just bought me this new bed that had been smashed to bits.

DB: *So what did you say to them?*

STUDENT 4: I told the truth, because I knew that somehow they would understand.

DB: *You must have very fine parents.*

STUDENT 4: They're great.

Interacting with the story

When students read a story, it is the dynamic of narrative that propels them forward. Often in school, we stress the ability to analyse once the story is read, rather than the skills of making meaning while reading. Of course, teachers who are helping students learn to read adopt strategies that help the students work inside the print mode, as they experience the words. Drama can nurture this ability.

Would you rather . . .
Your dad did a dance at school
or your mom had a fight in a cafe?

These two images usually take the student on a different journey.

In drama, there is the self that one begins with and the other that one takes on. At times, the self is the motive force of the drama, dictating words and action from personal background and from a particular value system; at other times, the adopted persona is dominant, presenting a complex subject to explore through talk and drama. Role is the juxtaposition of these two parts, so that the learning is viewed internally, but from a new or different perspective.

In working with these choices concerning parents, I found that the responses were filtered through students' personal experiences. Those who imagined their dads doing a dance at school had interesting reasons: he did it to raise money for the Home and School Association, cheer up a class that had done poorly on a test, or take part in an ethnic festival's activities. No one was embarrassed; everyone seemed to think that it would be a positive experience for both the dad and the class. However, when students depicted, in small groups, a mother's fight in a restaurant, there were many conflicting emotions, most of them centring on the mother. Many students in their reconstructions defended the mother's actions, but all were embarrassed.

STUDENT: We were in the McDonald's restaurant. My mother was in line, when suddenly a man butted in front of her. Right away, my mother's lover came up and told that guy to get back into line . . .

Story after story concerned wrongs being righted, emotions overruling reason, families disagreeing. The scene triggered the playing out of many stored-up tensions. The self and the other were melding, and the students found themselves united in their feelings about the arguments. This intersection of the students' private worlds and the world of the story produces power for building comprehension and response. A resonant relationship is set up between the individual responses of the students and the story. The students begin interacting with the story in ever-widening ways, adding to their childhood gardens an awareness of the lives of other classmates, the world of the author, and their newfound perceptions in role. (Burningham's Everychild is shown to be embarrassed in each situation.)

Developing stories from settings

In a regular class with time to develop the situations, each of the ideas can be the beginning of a full-fledged drama lesson as well as a stimulus for word play and dramatic brainstorming.

Would you rather be lost . . .
In the fog, at sea,
in a desert,

in a forest
or in a crowd . . .

The dramas that have grown out of these settings have varied widely with the interests of the group. We have discovered missing cities arising from the mists of the past. We have been in lifeboats lost on the sea and have found an island from *Lord of the Flies*. We have searched for water in a desert, only to find it was controlled by an evil king. We have found in the forest a society of people who have lived underground for their entire lives. We have been lost in a crowd of aliens, unable to reveal our true identities until we could find someone we knew to be trustworthy.

Would you rather . . .
Your house was surrounded by water,
snow
or jungle

A Grade 1 class had chosen their environments. Each child was demonstrating the difficulties and pleasures of a particular setting, and I was observing them and gently prodding them with specific questions about the nature of their lifestyles. A child with Down's syndrome was making angels in the snow, and, unsure of his abilities, I began asking him questions.

DB: *Is your house surrounded by snow?*
The child nodded affirmatively.
DB: *Do you like living here in the snow?*
The child again nodded yes.
DB: *Are you the King of Winter?*
The child nodded yes.
DB: *Then what are you wearing on your head?*
CHILD: A crown of ice.

Reflection

I want students to wear crowns of ice in summer, have eagles steal their vegetables, let hippos sleep in their beds, take breakfast in balloons. As also, I am certain, would John Burningham.

Encouraging Dramatic Play

Play is vital to the development of students. We watch as they grow and learn spontaneously in their play time—talking, developing their imaginations, ordering and making sense of their experiences through their own observations and impressions. Many Kindergarten and Grade 1 classrooms have facilities that encourage dramatic play, ranging from a Drama centre to a well-equipped room or area. Materials such as boxes, cloaks, hats, tools and models can often stimulate undirected play. Some teachers assign groups to certain areas, such as a Cooking centre, in order to encourage role playing; others may allow dramatic play as a response

Watching my five-year-old son talk to himself in play made me realize the importance of play exploration in language development. Through projected play in which he manipulated and gave voice to toy symbols and through dramatic play in which he himself was inside the medium of drama, he used words and registers unavailable to him in non-play situations. Every aspect of language was investigated: he played multiple roles, changing at rapid-fire speed, adapting his voice qualities to the demands of a particular character, and altering syntax to fit the situation. He was inside the play looking at his own creations as spectator, and refocusing and elaborating where and when necessary.

When my four-year-old son role-played "Snow White" with me over a period of months, he reminded me at all times to "stick to the story," not to elaborate or extend the details, and to work within his predetermined ritualistic confines. Only when he entered Kindergarten did he begin to allow "what if" to creep into the play. When, as the witch, he asked me as Snow White if I wanted an apple, I could at last reply, "No thanks, but I would enjoy a juicy ripe pear," and he in turn could say, "I just happen to have a pear right here in my basket. Try biting the bright yellow inside." It was a new Snow White story, and he and I were engaged in versioning, in creating our own fairy tale within a structured drama context.

to a story, a discussion, or a particular theme. Of course, students beyond Grade 1 need "play" to become healthy adults, and our drama events can offer them opportunities to live in pretend ways, as imagined others for a period of time. Valued by school and supported by curriculum outcomes, dramatic play is validated as authentic learning.

As teachers, we can facilitate the dramatic play environment, helping students expand their themes and extending and supplementing the language and the play with appropriate attitudes, approaches, and strategies. We can guide the action, encourage particular activity, question the students about what is happening, and even enter the play situation by taking on a role ourselves.

Observation of student play can help us plan lessons based on their experiences for the time when we introduce them to directed activities in drama. We can find, in undirected activities, new directions for more formal drama lessons which will help students experiment, consider alternatives, work in groups, and order their ideas. As Richard Courtney pointed out, though, much dramatic play takes place outside the control of the teacher.

Three ways to foster dramatic play

These three examples should prompt further ideas about how to engage students in dramatic play.

A dangerous creature: A large creature was constructed from cardboard boxes by a Kindergarten class, and, after discussion, was tethered to a table because it was fiery. It became a source of interest and concern for the students, who decided that it required feeding at intervals and arranged for keepers to do this. The keepers would discuss what to give and how much. Over a period the creature stimulated many other play activities, leading students into discussion, art, and writing (students' oral language being written in a large class book by their teachers).

A strange planet: Five-year-old children spread physical education hoops and blocks on the floor to create another planet, which they then explored as space travellers from a "Skytrek" craft. They worked fairly independently, but kept within a broad plan of agreement and used technical terms like *astronaut*, *module*, and *linkup* in their language exchanges. Movement showed an awareness of the space environment chosen, and afterwards their teacher commented on the obvious influence of television programs. Students managed to sustain the activity for some time through co-operative endeavor and suggestions.

A giant's castle: A group of seven-year-olds established a giant's castle using assorted large cardboard boxes and then enjoyed a series of short adventures in which the giant was taunted. Discussion centred on who should act as giant next and the content of various action sequences, with most children making contributions. Several imaginative possibilities were suggested and explored, including a ghost sequence intended to frighten the giant from his castle. Two children exerted an obvious influence on the remainder of the group, and there seemed to be tacit agreement between them on who would lead at different times.

Demonstration: Beyond Play Time—Finding Common Ground

I was working with a group of teachers in a summer program where we were to engage a Kindergarten class in a structured drama experience and analyse the teaching techniques used as the work progressed. Four teachers began the work, involving 30 children in creating a play park. The children sang camp songs, told of favorite park activities, and then in small groups began to mime the use of play equipment, locating the park in time and space within the classroom. Each group described or demonstrated its playground creations to other groups.

Encountering a threat: As this was happening, a teacher in role, wearing a safety helmet, was posting signs around the room: "Playground to be closed and replaced with a building." Eventually, the children began to notice the signs, and those who could read told the others about the impending development. The children began to stop their park play. They complained vehemently to the teacher in role as park supervisor that their park should not be destroyed for a building. I focused the discussion on what could be done and the children made posters of protest, which they later mounted over the signs. They also composed a collective letter of complaint to the mayor. Then the lesson stopped for the day.

Considering alternatives: At the next session, the children began by singing their camp songs, followed by a brief discussion reviewing the previous lesson's proceedings. The class was divided into four small groups with one teacher/leader per group, to air and solidify the children's objections to the building. The whole class gathered to confront one teacher in role as a city planner, who explained that a home for senior citizens was to be built on the park land. The children presented their arguments, and the planner was sympathetic, but firmly stated the project was going ahead.

A teacher re-entered in the role of Mrs. Marshall, an older woman who wanted to move into the new building. As the children questioned her, they began to examine the necessity for the building on the park land. The teacher in role refocused the energies of the class towards alternatives to the confrontation, using ideas from the children to "build" a drama. Mrs. Marshall revealed that the home she was leaving had a large lot attached to it, and she would be willing to donate this lot to the city as a playground. The children accepted this as a satisfactory solution. They re-established the playground in the new area through action and words, with the teachers in role as playground supervisors. In a sense, they ended where they had begun.

Reflection

Two aspects of these lessons stand out as particularly significant: the change in the direction of the drama when the children recognized the signs' implications for their fictional playground, and the shift in tension and feeling when they understood Mrs. Marshall's need for a new home. They had moved through dramatic play to group consensus in a reflective mode. They were not just demanding their own rewards, but considering and comprehending the needs of others.

Years ago, my friend David Davis, from England, was visiting me with his five-year-old daughter, Elaine. I was captivated by her ability to role-play with him as they re-created "Little Red Riding Hood." I managed to find, at her request, a basket and a tea towel to hide the goodies. It was with obvious delight that she took part in the familiar, yet always new dramatization, and her father was able to present a wonderfully vile wolf. When it was suggested that I portray the wolf in play with the child, I took the chance, and the dramatic play began as before. I followed her lead, maintaining the story. The work progressed until I said, "The better to see you with." At this moment, Elaine turned to her father and said that she didn't want to play anymore—the dramatic play had disappeared with the sudden reality of the situation.

This type of emotional and cognitive experiencing, followed by reflective distancing, is the hallmark of drama. In this kind of work, the play roots of the drama lesson are clearly in evidence—the children were very close to being themselves, working with familiar situations and attitudes. Then, they gradually adopted roles as determined by the situation. When the children who read the signs said, "They're going to get rid of the park," the role playing and the drama began.

Demonstration: From Lead Smelters to Desert Sheep—Journeying Together

I visited a Grade 2 class in an inner-city school, surrounded by lead smelters and all types of pollution. The principal had requested my help in bringing a drama program to the students to give them images other than the view from the school's grimy windows. I don't know why I chose an old biblical story. Perhaps I needed extra strength to walk through those doors into a fogged-in school. Clyde Robert Bulla's illustrations of Joseph and his family are dark and full of mystery, and they challenged my own understanding of the story. I wanted these students to work as one, and I created Jacob and his "32 children" as a setting for the drama, in a time and place far from their city.

We built a desert community, and they chose sheep and goats to herd. We found an oasis, cleared the sand, built troughs for water for the animals, and passed around a basket of dates to taste—real fruit that added a reality base to the drama. We then had a visit from the patriarch Jacob (myself in role) and a student in role as his favorite son, Joseph.

"My sons," I said, "you have worked well. Tomorrow, Joseph here will return with fresh fruit and wine to cool you in this heat. It is almost time to return to the settlement for the fall season. I look forward to having my sons around me again. And do you like Joseph's new coat? I made it myself. Strange how my skills as a tentmaker have come in so handy. I bid you farewell."

In a circle, Jacob's children told stories of their work and the heat and the soft life led by Joseph; their anger grew and they plotted to get rid of him. I had not read them the story, but drawing from memories of it and from folklore, they decided to sell him to traders. This was accomplished through mime with me in role as an Egyptian trader. Then it was time to go home to Jacob.

DB: *I am so happy my sons are back. Is Joseph arriving later?*
STUDENT 1: Joseph isn't coming.
DB: *Has he been detained?*
STUDENT 2: He can't come.
DB: *Why not?*
STUDENT 1: He's dead.
DB: *What do you mean, he's dead?*
STUDENT 1: He was killed.
DB: *How was he killed?*
STUDENT 1: By a sheep.
DB: *And how did a sheep kill him?*

Two tales of the desert are *Joseph the Dreamer* by Clyde Robert Bulla, featured here, and *One Night: A Story from the Desert* by Cristina Kessler and Ian Schoenherr.

STUDENT 3: It smothered him to death.
DB: *My son, smothered to death by a sheep!*
And no one laughed or spoke.

Reflection

The first boy brought meaning to the fictional situation, using the context we had built, the milieu of shepherds in the desert. He couldn't think of any dangers to Joseph other than sheep, and the second student supported him: to maintain the drama, he decided on the spot that the essence of sheep was wool and all wool could do was smother. By accepting their belief rather than questioning it, I could continue the drama.

The honesty of these students' struggle is the quality of education that I am after. Give me sheep as killers any day instead of surface, glib answers provided for the amusement of all. I am impressed with the struggle, with the journey. Thirty-two children in my tent, and we understood Jacob, Joseph, and the brothers.

Later in the day, I watched the children in the playground. Their small bodies seemed as grey as the tarmac, but they ran with urchin energy, and as their words filtered up to my classroom window, I realized they were chasing one boy and shouting, "Get Joseph! Get Joseph!"

Oh, that fabled coat of many colors!

Demonstration: Belief in the Wolf Boy—Moving into Drama

These titles all explore the notion of wolf children:

Children of the Wolf by Jane Yolen
The Wolf Girls by Jane Yolen & Heidi Elisabeth Stemple
The Wild Boy by Mordecai Gerstein
Victor by Mordecai Gerstein

For several hundred years, there have been reports of children who have been reared in the wild by animals or kept isolated from all social contact. Sometimes, the information is based on little more than a brief press report. At other times, the cases have been studied in detail, particularly the stories of Victor, Kaspar Hauser, Amala and Kamala, and Genie.

During one summer session, I invited a Grade 4 class identified as having behavioral problems to take part in our program. I chose Jane Yolen's *Children of the Wolf* to work with.

The students sat on a rug in front of me and the teachers in a semi-circle behind them. I began with a discussion of books and films they had read, seen, or heard about concerning children raised by creatures of the jungle or the forest. The class recalled Tarzan, Mowgli, and a wolf child remembered from past experiences.

I then presented the students with the problem to be solved through drama: "We are a group of scientists who have been awarded the contract for developing a program for humanizing a 12-year-old boy, discovered living in a forest and raised by wolves. In four years, we are to create a civilized 16-year-old who will have a chance at a normal life. The first step for our group is to create a set of priorities concerning the training of the wolf boy."

Working in small groups in role as scientists, the students considered the various problems that confronted them in changing the feral child's behavior and inculcating human values. Different groups developed strategies for working on the wolf boy's language, clothing, food, education, social habits, and emotional needs. The small groups then presented their ideas to the whole class who, along with me in a neutral role as director of the project, questioned them and offered suggestions. The students were building a belief in the existence of the wolf boy, and as the members of each group processed the contributions of the class and altered their plans, they were using "talk in role" as their medium for learning.

Presenting findings: I then telescoped time by announcing that one year had passed, and each group must reveal the progress they had made with the wolf boy. The language of the students dramatically changed as the groups presented their findings. They took their roles as scientists seriously, using their notes from clipboards that I had distributed to each group as the basis for their discussion. Their body language, choice of words, sense of audience, and strength in role became much more complex. They seemed to think of themselves as authorities, as their commitment to the drama grew.

Arguing about what's best: Later still, when I asked them to present their findings at the end of the third year of their experiments, the first group announced that they felt the boy should be freed to return home. Their proclamation divided the class, and we separated into two large groups, representing the two sides of the issue: should he remain or be freed? Emotions were strong, resulting in a third group who were undecided and stood between the other two groups. The arguing continued, and those in the middle found themselves joining with whoever was speaking at the moment.

Unfortunately, the school bus arrived and there was no completion to the drama, but the teacher had the students write me letters describing their feelings, and the following excerpts represent the range of opinions that grew from the work.

> *I think he should be a boy.*
>
> *It was confusing to decide if he should be a boy or a wolf. It was hard, but I think that he should be a wolf.*
>
> *I like the story about the wolf-boy, and I said the wolf-boy should have cooked food and the scientists said the wolf-boy should be in a white room to be studied and see how to eat the raw meat.*
>
> *Thank you for inviting us to hear the story about the wolf boy. We had fun as scientists. I think we should leave him a wolf boy because he don't see no one to tell him something about people.*
>
> *It was a very interesting morning. I enjoyed myself a lot. It was real exciting. I also learned a great deal. It was a great experience for me and I will never forget that day.*
>
> *And let the wolf boy make his own choice.*

Reflection

The students and I never saw the wolf boy or had anyone try to play him in role: there seemed no need for his presence. The class talked about him and created him in his absence. They cared passionately about his past and argued with conviction about his future. Their language grew with the situation and with their belief in the wolf child. In role they were scientists who had begun to wear the mantle of the expert: they controlled the direction of the drama and the quality of the language. They had ownership of their work.

Demonstration: The Wolf Boy's Plea—Playing Experts

I chose the same beginning structure with a Grade 8 gifted class. I shared the cover of Jane Yolen's novel and we settled on the central questions of the drama: "Which is the boy—wolf or human? What makes us human?"

Once again, I presented the problem: they had to civilize the wolf boy in four years and at the end of each year, I would ask for a report. In each report, groups of anthropologists, sociologists, and others had to discuss possibilities, organize priorities, synthesize opinions, and finally stand and give an oral summary. Based on what they reported, I called for a little more.

• If the wolf boy were given a pet by the scientists and got along with the pet, I asked that they try him with humans.

• If he was using a toilet, but soiling his bedding once in a while, I asked that this problem be solved by the next year.

At the end of the third year, I informed the group that the boy was to appear on national television. The students in role as scientists announced that they were apprehensive because the wolf boy's behavior was still unpredictable. I suggested that they medicate the boy for the appearance and they agreed. When one student questioned this approach, I said they must do this if the boy was to appear on television. I was testing to see if the moral issue would be picked up by the group, but it was not; however, I knew the issue could be returned to later during reflection time.

Finally, the wolf boy was ready to be presented. He was "human" according to the scientists and could appear on national television, communicating in an intelligent way with other human beings. The students as scientists had a strong sense of accomplishment. According to their reports, at the end of four years, the boy's wildness was apparently eliminated, and he was ready to join human society.

The significance of decisions: It was time to reintroduce the questions that had begun the drama. I chose to work as teacher in role, to role-play the wolf boy who was now, in appearance and behavior, a civilized human being. Speaking to the scientists gathered together, I asked to be returned to my "home"—the wolf pack. The students as scientists had to rethink their answers to the original questions: "Which is the boy—wolf or human? What makes us human?" They had worked confidently for their "project leader," by using their knowledge of social sciences to civilize the wolf boy, and now he was saying to them, with the very words they had given him: "I want to go home." I asked those who would help me to step forward; then turned to each of those who would not and asked why not. At this point the drama was at its most intense.

Some students individually faced the wolf boy and began to realize the significance of their decision, whether it was to return him to the pack or keep him in human society. It became a lesson where the power of the work touched each participant, and what the students felt was depicted in their words, their faces, and their actions.

Reflection

Demands, especially of a technical kind, can elevate the situation. In this lesson, the students were "specialists" and used technical language befitting their roles. I acted as a manager to whom they had to explain the situation, elevating their language in order to help them explain their success. The emphasis was not on the accuracy of the vocabulary, but on the general tone with which the students spoke. Their expert roles were enhanced because they were explaining to someone less knowledgeable than themselves their contribution to the educational program. Thus, the type of language demanded was always within their grasp. By controlling the knowledge, they were learning not only about the drama, but about the power of talk itself.

The Need to Let Students Talk

Dear Mr. Booth,

I really enjoyed talking about the wolf boy. (Even if I pretty well thought it wasn't true.) It was a very interesting subject. Although I am a shy person, I didn't talk much but enjoyed listening to others while having a bunch of thoughts whizzing through my head.

Yours truly,
Jennifer

During the wolf boy lesson, as Jennifer was speaking in role, the classroom teacher had whispered in my ear, "She has never spoken in class." But as Jennifer's letter indicates, her own awareness of her shyness, her inability to talk in public, did not limit her learning. And when the context was strong enough, as in the drama moment, she could and would speak.

As valuable as the thought and language that occur in the drama may be, the thought and language that occur afterwards may be as important. While drama is an active, "doing" medium, reflecting on what happened presents a powerful way for students to make meaning. They can examine and understand their thoughts and perceptions, both as spectators and as participants. The students, discussing collaboratively as a whole class or in small groups or writing in personal journals, can look back on what they have done.

We want the students to ponder and consider the implications of what is happening within the drama. As Dorothy Heathcote puts it, they need to "stumble upon authenticity in their work" and to experience and reflect upon their experience. Whatever techniques the teacher uses to promote reflection, they must not interfere with the drama as perceived by the students.

Reflective discussion lets students revisit and rethink their thoughts and observations about the issues and concerns raised in the drama. Students begin to think aloud, to grapple with the language they need to express their evolving ideas, to clarify and change their opinions. They seek to explain the motives and behavior shown during the drama, finding reasons and implications for the assumptions and decisions they made.

As teachers, we can question and deepen their ideas, giving them opportunities to make explicit the learning that occurred. (Sometimes, students will be so involved with the drama that they discuss what happened in the drama while remaining in role.) As we and our students engage in talk, we literally tell the stories of our lives as we live them, constructing the realities of our beings in conversation. As individuals, we must assimilate our experiences and build them into a continuing picture of our world. The responses we get through talk profoundly affect both the world picture we are creating and our view of ourselves. All talk, be it purposeful or random in nature, helps us look at the human race in all its variety, and is therefore educative.

We need to let students talk, in and out of role, and we need to engage in conversations with them, adding our voices to the classroom sounds of learning.

Chapter 2: Involving the Students in Planning for Story Drama

Jerome Bruner suggests that "the shrewd guess, the fertile hypothesis, the courageous leap to a tentative conclusion—these are the most valuable coin of the thinker at work, whatever his line of work." For this to happen, for students' thinking and feeling skills to be sharpened and used in story drama, a teacher's intervention is necessary, mandatory, and a vital part of the teaching/learning process.

Structuring for Spontaneity and Learning

As a teacher, I move the students into areas of significance where they will be challenged to learn. I cannot detract from their part in shaping the drama, but rather must build upon it. I try to see the implications of every suggestion and then find an appropriate strategy for using the ideas for the larger, overall education goals of the group.

There will, of course, be times when students will engage in drama in a spontaneous and open-ended structure, maintaining the "as if" situation and developing the action without intervention. Working in a play mode, they may resent being moved into a more structured way of learning with a focus that attempts to unite the whole group. They may need time to work this way for a while, continuing to build physical belief in the drama situation, concretizing the details and the environment. However, students may also require structures that enable their feelings and responses to be explored, clarified, modified, and transformed into something that can be understood and reflected upon.

As a story drama facilitator, I need to set up learning structures that allow for the spontaneity of the students, but that engage them in a meaningful learning experience, that encourage them to explore rather than to demonstrate what they know. I need to choose activities within the abilities of the group, yet stretch their developing capacities. I need to create learning atmospheres where talk is healthy and normal, so that I can elicit constant response and support the contributions of each student. I need to challenge superficial responses and press for students to elaborate and extend weak contributions, but do so without rejecting the speakers themselves. I need to seek further information from the class without burdening them with my own knowledge. I need to use various modes of teaching to pace the work so that feelings and thoughts are encouraged to develop, carefully observing which attitudes and perceptions should be

My job is to help the students find a drama focus acceptable to the majority of the class, not to direct the drama or just have the students follow orders. I try not to provide answers, but instead direct the situation, applying pressure and deepening the experience where necessary. It is a continual process of organization and reorganization, of focusing and refocusing.

focused upon, and which are detrimental. These needs and concerns are true for all story drama facilitators.

The right choice and management of situations, contexts, and stories relating to the environment, for instance, can provide young people with authentic experiences of how they would find it to be in surroundings far removed in time and place from their own. Drama deals with concrete and specific contexts, particular people in a particular relationship in a particular place at a particular time. Teachers need to take into account the nature of the students, their experience, their needs, their abilities, and their interests. They must choose from a repertoire of drama techniques and strategies, employing each drama convention towards the building of the collaborative drama activity.

See *The Art of Drama Teaching* by Michael Fleming for more.

Working Alongside the Students

When they work in role alongside students in building fictional worlds, teachers alter their status in the classroom. Students can then communicate with teachers and with each other in ways very different from those in real life in the classroom setting. Teachers, of course, still retain control of the classroom, but the drama and the roles determine the direction of the work. If the teacher is an adviser to the king who is in reality a student, then it is the student as king who will determine the fate of the village. This altering of the dynamic of the interaction between teacher and student—the tone, the register, the choice of words, the implication of the speech—can give great freedom and strength to the voices of the students; it can also allow the teacher to extend the type of talk in which students engage.

The relationship between the teacher and the class is often different in a drama lesson than in other types of lessons. Rather than suppressing activity, the teacher invites and encourages physical and verbal activity, containing students' contributions within a meaningful framework. The students should feel adventurous and creative, yet work within the rules of the classroom. It is important that the teacher understand his or her own security threshold, attitudes to drama, and the need to retain control of the lesson—story drama work may last as little as five minutes or as long as a month.

Co-operative interaction is an important aspect of drama. Such interaction relies on respecting each member's unique and honest contribution, developing mutual trust which facilitates individual growth, building a climate of acceptance—of social, emotional, psychological, and physical freedom—and keeping open communication between student and student and teacher and student. The effective teacher encourages the sincere and honest expression of ideas and feelings.

Providing scope for commitment

In story drama, the best control device is to provide content that students will find interesting and relevant, and that will lead to their own work. If it is to be successful, a drama experience needs to offer students scope for emotional commitment and aesthetic satisfaction.

Students learn best when they feel committed, when they together decide to take up a challenge and reach a goal. Doing this requires that they understand and accept the plan for solving the dramatic problem. If they contribute to the planning—and if the teacher demonstrably takes account of their contributions—the students will come to own the drama. Some form of negotiation or consultation is therefore essential for developing commitment and learning. The students should be encouraged both to make independent decisions and realize the consequences of those decisions. The process of thinking through an idea and experimenting by trial and error helps them learn to make their own choices.

Exercising control techniques

It takes time to learn how to manage an interactive and improvisational drama experience. These suggestions may help.

- A circle is an excellent control technique. The teacher has a total view of the class and can speak to each student across the circle. There is a unity to the group, everyone is equal in the space, and the centre of the circle can become an immediate area for demonstration.

- A signal for freezing will also aid in controlling a class. For example, a tambourine can be struck or rattled to indicate that the group should stand still, frozen to the spot. This signal must not be overused, but can help improve the students' concentration.

- Asking the students to work in slow motion, as in a dream, may help control movement, improve concentration, and increase involvement.

- Intervening, arresting, or stopping the action of the drama allows the teacher to clarify the instructions, define or redefine the focus, build belief, achieve a consensus within the group, deal with conflicting emotions, or allow time for reflection.

- Replaying a drama lesson allows new ideas to be added and encourages refining and polishing for a final synthesis of the ideas that have been explored. If sharing is a goal, the drama should be replayed with energy and new learning rather than as a rehearsed scene.

Helping Students Let Go of Disbelief

Some students can't believe in "the big lie," can't accept the magic "what if." They seem locked into their present reality—an imagined world is outside their ken. What are the blocks to their suspending disbelief, and how does this inability affect so much of what these students think about in all aspects of their lives? Is letting go of the "here and now" such a painful release? What do they feel they are hanging on to—image, self, past? And when they do take flight on drama wings, can they remain airborne?

Some students simply tag along until suddenly the situation, the tension, or the group pulls them inside the drama, and they begin to think "as if." Perhaps others need more formal approaches for allowing themselves to enter the imaginary garden. I wonder if they played as

---

Although we must care about self-expression, we must also be deeply concerned about development—cognitive, affective, and spiritual—in a social context, and not be averse to or afraid of setting up structures that help students in working in the experiential medium of drama, to gain control over it, to find new insights and make understandings.

Tony was 10 years old and couldn't find the sand in the desert—he only saw linoleum on the studio floor. "There ain't no sand! There ain't no desert!" No matter the framework of the lesson, Tony never left the actual space of the room. On parents' night, I usually demonstrated with the children as their parents watched, re-creating a piece of work they had explored, and using theatre crafts, such as lighting and masks, to heighten the experience. In a moment of darkness, Tony, who had in his generosity been going through the motions, turned to me and said, "Is that my mother sitting there?"
"Yes, Tony."
"Is this a play we're doing?"
"Yes, Tony."

preschool infants, if they saw only a sandbox and not a city, sat inside a cardboard carton and not a space capsule, baked play-dough circles and not pies. Or is it a rejection of play roles, a deliberate refusal to step back and look at life in a new way? How much trust in self does it take to creep into others' shoes, if only for 30 minutes while standing on linoleum in a faraway desert?

I have watched some adults—teachers—fight the big lie. Even though they know they are working in an art form that requires active participation, they hold back, either acting in a stereotypical manner or sabotaging the drama, unable to be part of the co-operative and celebratory activity, unable to live through a fictional, yet completely real, experience. Often, they tell me that nothing was happening, so they decided to instigate a new drama direction: they chose not to listen to and observe their fellow participants and let the power of the art build the framework. It is sometimes very difficult to fall voluntarily into the collective creation.

Because drama is a social process, the students should be concerned with the ideas of others, with fitting their own thoughts and feelings into the group effort. Through their interactions, both in and out of role, they negotiate for both shared and personal meanings, developing an awareness of form and control from inside the drama. But, as in their sandbox deserts, pretending must be "real."

Demonstration: Alone on an Island—Immersed in a Community

Several years ago, working with teachers and Inuit students, I was in Hudson Bay on a remote island called Sanikiluaq. I taught three groups, beginning with Kindergarten and moving to Grade 8. I had no idea I would find minus 40 degree weather on my arrival—I was just wearing a trench coat. When I met the Inuit parents, students, and leaders, they simply stared at me.

The leader of the community rose and said, "I wish to greet you, but I haven't your skill in languages and I shall struggle to speak in English and do my best." And he was, of course, a most eloquent speaker. He then made the same speech in Inuit and I was embedded in the community for two weeks. I went seal hunting, ice fishing, skidooing, partying—and I taught drama. If you ever want to throw yourself into using only what you are, try working in Hudson Bay.

When I walked into the first class of students, they all began speaking in Inuit among themselves, and I knew I was a foreigner, an alien, a stranger, a distrusted one. And I had no idea how to begin or where to start. Everything, every warm-up I've ever thought of, died in that minus 40 degree weather. (In the four minutes it took to get to the school, my glasses would frost over so heavily I had to scrape them before I could see.) I had brought my case of books, thinking I would begin with myths and legends, but none of them seemed to apply to where I was. I was trapped in this room. I decided to move right into drama.

"Tell me about your community," I said. And they all roared with laughter because it was only as big as the room, with 200 students and 300 adults. They had all known their community from the day they were born. And they had never left.

"Why do we want to bother taking time to talk about our community?" they asked.

"Because I'm a stranger and I want to know a little bit about it."

And so they began. We listed on the blackboard all the important places: the Hudson's Bay store, the co-op, the recreation centre, the school, the Mountie station, the nurse's clinic, and so on. Then I said, "If I were a government official sent to your community to eliminate one service building, which one would you choose?" They had a discussion for an hour and a half. I watched girls who could not speak to me begin whispering to one another across the room. We began discussing the buildings, one by one, until we had a consensus: only the Hudson's Bay store was erased. I was in the middle of their drama, totally controlled by them, using all the strategies I'd learned in my world. From then on, I had no trouble.

After the final gathering at the teacher's house, a group of Inuit constructed an icehouse for me, an igloo, built into the ground. They put a lamp in it, and I entered the house as it glowed from the inside. It was such a powerful place. I felt the North around me, inside me. Later, when I was walking home, there was no wind and the stars were out. It was breathtaking, free of all urban industrial grime.

And at midnight, in the middle of this island, in the middle of Hudson Bay, on a snow-covered hill, I heard a 14-year-old Inuit youth, all by himself, singing Bruce Springsteen's "Born in the USA." I realized that I had been there, on their island, trying to learn about them, and for decades popular culture had been filtering, even flooding into their world. That boy wasn't singing to me, he was singing to himself and to the spirits of his island. He was in the middle of a theatre experience. He was full of drama, and I was moved.

Finding the Drama

Basically, drama is an art form that examines problems in a special way. By working through the issues of a theme being explored in drama, as teacher, you are able to see all of the concerns from *inside* the drama, feeling and thinking about a theme from the viewpoint of someone involved in the action as it happens. Everything you do or say affects the drama and affects all the participants' views on what is being examined. It is as if you are watching yourself in a play at the same time as the play is happening. You are physically and emotionally involved, and yet you are able to analyse what is going on.

Finding the drama usually happens after much exploration work. The group must always work at focusing and directing the action. Problems or difficulties arising during the drama work can sometimes be worked through in role without stopping the action. At other times, the drama will have to be stopped and the difficulties sorted out through discussion. When a group is able to build on a single focus, when all the participants are fully in role, and when everyone is committed to making the drama happen, then finding the drama will be inevitable. Most of the work in drama concerns finding that moment when understanding strikes, when we learn about the situation and about ourselves.

In drama, the students are allowed to talk themselves into believing in the fiction, to hear their ideas bounced back, to reframe and refocus their own information and attitudes, to recognize the need for communicating what they believe to those who believe differently, to hear language at work. Their words sweep them into thought, and as they recognize the truth of what they are saying, that very language is transformed into new patterns. It determines the action and lets them see the impact, all while they are in the midst of the action, in the eye of the hurricane.

Although drama operates in a fictional setting, it must never be done in a "pretend" way, or the feelings that students express will not be truly felt. The more honestly students can respond to the situation, the more they will be drawn into their roles—thinking, feeling, and interacting within the drama. If students discover their roles from inside the drama activity, then those roles will grow from within; they will not be something put on from the outside, like a costume. Being part of a role that has been created in this way will help them believe in the drama and help them remain committed to its development. In this way, the drama can be built up over a series of lessons so that the students' commitment to the work will grow, as well.

Seeking the authentic

It is important to help students avoid dramatic clichés and stereotypes. Clichés are pre-set responses to dramatic situations. For example: Suppose you received a letter containing bad news. The dramatic cliché would be to gasp, clasp your forehead, and move about in a distraught manner. In real life, however, different people would react in different ways to this situation.

In drama, we are asked to find the appropriate response for the role that we are playing: one that is thoughtful and that allows us in role to express our own responses to such situations. We are asked to go beyond the superficial and to discover the human qualities of our roles. By working from inside themselves to find their roles, students may understand how to build a character in drama. By listening and responding to others in the group, and by taking the time to work through the problems of building belief in their roles, they will gain opportunities to create powerful drama.

Teacher Roles in Building Drama

Teacher as instructor: As part of regular classroom interaction, the teacher can ask questions, discuss, control, contribute, and clarify before the drama begins, when the action of the drama stops, and during post-drama reflection time. All useful teacher knowledge needs to be applied to every drama event.

Teacher as narrator: This is such a useful strategy, for the teacher can do so many things by simply saying, "I remember when." When I review my notes, I can find many examples of the ways I have furthered the drama as narrator, including the following:

- when I set the mood (e.g., "The cave is growing dark. Now there is no light of any kind. Shadows loom over the lonely tribe, huddled together.")

- when I cover jumps in time (e.g., "What will happen 10 years from now when the tribe meets a stranger who has never heard of its problems?")

- when I prepare the students for what will come next (e.g., "Each member of the tribe went to his or her small private place in the cave and began to think about the past 10 years, the losses, the pain, the incidents that couldn't be forgotten.")

- when I incorporate details necessary for the drama (e.g., "Each member of the tribe votes by selecting a black or white pebble and placing the pebble, after careful consideration, in the hidden space by the door.")

- when I make the students aware of how they have changed (e.g., "The members of the tribe lie around the fire, understanding that now they solve problems not through war but through negotiation and arbitration.")

- when I give import to the words and actions of the students (e.g., "The tribe agrees to be governed by the dictates of the council, to accept the legislated decisions, and to comply with the requests of the chosen body.")

- when I present stories from my own life (e.g., "I remember when . . . ")

Teacher as side-coach: After I saw how the British educator David Davis coached students in his youth theatre from the North of England, helping them to extend awareness of their roles, to deepen their interpretations, to consider how an audience would grasp how and why they were living through the scene, I made coaching my main mode of working in drama with youngsters.

As side-coach, the teacher can give encouraging or descriptive commentary as the students take part in drama as a group or as a whole class. By suggesting actions and ideas the students might explore, the teacher can help sustain the drama's momentum. Sometimes, only a few students need side-coaching; sometimes, the whole class requires it. The teacher's voice can give confidence to nervous or insecure students or inject enthusiasm into a lacklustre activity. The teacher can remind the students of ideas mentioned in discussion that could now be incorporated. The suggestions should be tentative, and teacher should not attempt to impose ideas on the group. When side-coaching, the teacher must go where needed, encourage the less sure, point out story ideas, convey approval, and, in general, give reinforcement constantly.

Teacher in role: The teacher works inside the drama, alongside the students, and stays in role until students need to process the information the drama has so far given them or examine the directions the drama might now take. The teacher may need to adopt more than one role during the lesson in order to satisfy the needs of the drama. Here are some types of roles that the teacher may choose from:

- the antagonist (Mayor: "Who will pay the taxes to keep the orphanage open?")

- the helper (Wizard: "May I give you three magic spells to help you on the journey?")

- the leader (King: "You people must move your homes nearer the river.")

- the interrogator (Warden: "Who is responsible for this commotion?")

- the interviewer (Reporter: "When did you first notice the trouble?")

- the seeker of information (Stranger: "Can anyone here tell me why we have been banned from the village?")

Choice is governed by what the teacher wants to accomplish.

Working successfully in role does not require great acting skill on the part of the teacher; rather, it depends on adopting a set of attitudes. The students must know when the teacher is and is not in role—perhaps the teacher could sit in a particular spot when stopping the drama or engaging in discussion. However, the teacher needs to transmit signals that indicate full belief in the role being played and in the dramatic situation. I have never maintained a role for a whole lesson.

When working in role, I can open up a number of routes for enriching the drama.

- I can extend the drama from within the drama process.

- I can challenge the class in ways not possible as teacher, by being aggressive, supporting a minority view, moving the drama along, or suggesting alternatives.

- I can elevate the language, support the contributions of the students, stand in the way of silly solutions, or slow down the action of the drama for clarification.

I recommend the resource *Role Reconsidered: A Re-evaluation of the Relationship between Teacher-in-role and Acting* by Judith Ackroyd.

Working in role with the whole class allows me to guide the students in using the art form of drama; then, they can apply this learning when they work in small groups. If I need to focus the class's attention, I can be an old, wise elder, reminding them of the past. If I need to energize the group, I can present new information that endangers their prosperity. If I need to quieten them down, I can ask them in role to come one by one to me, as the scribe of the village, to record their deepest questions. This teaching repertoire allows me to operate in a useful frame with a group of students.

A most useful role in working alongside students is the shadow role, as described by Dorothy Heathcote. The teacher is inside the drama, assisting the students and structuring the work from an indirect, non-specific role, such as a villager like everybody else, or a member of the community; however, the teacher represents a committed and dedicated role player. In truth, this is much like side-coaching in a traditional drama class, where we gently help the students focus and frame their ideas. This shadow role, of course, can merge into other categories, such as a teacher working in a lower status role, bringing information, or reflecting back to the students stories from past experiences with similar conflicts. In the last few years, this is the role I find myself using in drama events. It seems to offer the students maximum support within the context of the drama.

Demonstration: Four Mining Towns—Constructing Drama Events

When students work from realistic fiction, their research in print and on the Internet can provide the drama with powerful and deepening information. Examples of realistic fiction include

Boy of the Deeps by Ian Wallace
The Gift Stone by Robyn Eversole
In Coal Country by Judith Hendershot

I had the good fortune of giving a workshop in Austria for teachers interested in drama in education. The delegates were from several countries, including Austria, Germany, Hungary, the Czech Republic, and Slovenia. As the sessions developed, these delegates revealed their depth of experience in both drama and in the aesthetic knowledge that makes drama experiences powerful.

Using the picture book *Boy of the Deeps* by Ian Wallace as a shared beginning, each of four groups examined life in a fictitious American mining town in the 1940s. Despite their different home countries, participants chose issues and roles that allowed them to move beyond stereotypes into examining character relationships. I worked with each of the groups for a day, and each day the group participants selected the roles they wanted to portray in the drama. Each group invented a completely different scenario through their improvised interactions in role, but all of them drew upon their personal images of what life could have been like in that town. Consequently, each of the four towns began to take on a life of its own, populated by students, teenagers, miners (working, retired, or injured), widows and wives, grandmothers and grandfathers, store owners and store clerks, priests and ministers, mine owners, social workers, bar maids and barons, poets and journalists, cleaning ladies and nurses.

- Group one's drama revolved around a party dress that the daughter of a mining family, struggling with poverty, wanted for a dance. How the different members of the town reacted to her situation resulted in the building of the drama.

- Group two's session focused on an accident that had befallen one of the miners, resulting in a long-term stay in hospital, without health insurance. Complaints to the mine owner went nowhere, until the owner's wife became involved.

- Group three's drama grew into a complicated story about a priest who did not want to be assigned to a mining town, but who dreamed of living in Paris. A mentally challenged boy's plight changes the priest's life.

- Group four's work centred around a journalist who had come from Europe to write a profile of this mining town, and who ran into difficulty with the class distinctions that controlled the social nature of the community.

Reflection

How did these drama events take shape? What are the processes involved in directing and managing the action?

Building a drama event is a cumulative affair, like building a Lego model. Each scene grows from the stimulus of the preceding ones. In my mind, I keep track of what has already happened, so that I can begin another scene with a different context, drawing upon the energy and events of the previous one. When the mine owner tells about his difficulty with the miners, two or three miners might then comment on their treatment by the bosses; next, a miner's wife shares her life problems with her husband as she irons his Sunday shirt; then all the women of different ages meet at a quilting bee. I listen carefully to the improvised dialogue for entry points into the next incident. And scene upon scene, layer upon layer, the drama takes shape. We can also come back to a scene we have seen, or a character can offer another viewpoint. The action becomes layered with different meanings as the role players learn more and more about their lives in the town.

I see my roles in the making of the drama as a combination of several modes of working:

- the storyteller, who every so often narrates what has happened thus far and who needs the role players to fill in the gaps so the story builds its layers of meaning
  (*In this town, a young woman dreams of a party dress amid the greyness of daily life, but no one believes in her dream.*)

- the teacher-director, who prods and questions the players into rethinking and reconsidering the implications of their words and actions
  (*What are your thoughts about your injured husband not making any money to support you and your children? What will you not say to him?*)

- the teacher-manager, who organizes the brief scenes as they emerge from the talk and action of the role players, and who makes sure that different players have opportunities to respond to what has just happened
  (*As a parishioner, are you able to sense the priest's sense of failure? When you clean house for him, does he talk to you about his depression?*)

- the coach, who stands beside or behind hesitant players with suggestions or gentle questions, who projects them into the action of the play
  (*Tell about the accident when you lost your legs. Who helped you? Who told your wife?*)

- the role player, who occasionally works as a townsperson, commenting on or questioning another's actions or statements
  (*I give to the church from my pay pocket, and I am truly hurt by someone stealing money, even if it is to feed your children. What do the rest of you miners think?*)

Together in groups, the teachers and artists at this conference built their separate plays through interactive, improvised dialogue, with each group using the resources of its members. Although all their work began with the sharing of the same picture book, four unique representations of a mining town resulted. In the social conversations after the day's work, members of the different groups shared their drama adventures, often surprising and intriguing their colleagues with the differences in the four plays. As I write this brief description of four days of solid work, bits of their conversations appear in my teacher's mind, joining the ghost voices of all the lessons I have experienced—I am always shocked at the complexity of the drama participants, always surprised by the ones who plunge deepest into the story pool.

Postscript—Real Pretending

In summer 2005, in a course held in London, England, I used the same book, *Boy of the Deeps*, as a source for improvisation, but the drama evolved around the young lad who was beginning his life as a miner. We arranged a parent–teacher career night: five students role-played the principal and four teachers, and the rest were parents. The discussion revolved around one youth who wanted to leave school, even though he was eligible for a college scholarship. In role, the students commented on the different issues involved in his decision: speakers included his parents, saddened by his choice but supportive; a mine worker trumpeting the solidarity of miners; wives who had married at 16, some with and some without regrets; a mother who wanted her boy to get the scholarship now available; a mother saddened by her sense of being trapped in the village; new parents concerned about their child's stereotyped future; and teachers who felt they had done their best for the miners' children (and who all, when questioned by me, admitted they would never marry a miner).

The drama shone brightest, though, when one mother told of a wedding she had attended for her brother's son who was joining the military. She was asked what she wore to the ceremony, and she, with eyes shining, said: "A black and white polka dot dress with a red belt a white, wide-brimmed hat and white shoes. I looked good that day!"

All of us in London, two day after the bombing of the subways, were transported to a mining town that existed in our collective imagination. And two young women wept in real life. Drama is such real pretending.

Chapter 3: Exploring Stories through Dramatic Activities

How do we make drama happen? What techniques can we use to build its power, to increase its significance, so that the students participate willingly, work effectively in the art form, and recognize the value of their work?

The Basis of All Drama

Tension is the secret, the mystery, the surprise, the dangling carrot, the time frame, and the space limit. We need to apply pressures of some kind so that the students engaged in the drama will know the urgency of solving the problem or of making the decision at hand.

- We can introduce a surprising or shocking experience into the drama. For example, we can foreshadow that one of the people in the great canoe will die. The shock may force the students into rethinking what they were going to do.

- We can pull the experience in the opposite direction to where it seems to be going. In a plan where the class in role were to take over a community by appearing in the early morning fog, we tell them the fog has disappeared, the sky is clear, and we are in view of the enemy village.

- We can place special demands on the role players: they will have to solve a riddle so they can gain the right to speak to the wise one; they will have to speak in a way that the king will accept, using carefully chosen language to influence him.

- As teachers, we can make things difficult for the students: only one person knows the combination for the safe, or the swans will return earlier than normal because of the eclipse of the sun.

- We can also ask students to become the experts in a field: those who have information on a particular animal that is almost extinct, or those who understand a people's culture on an island we are about to visit.

- One of the most effective tensions is to slow down the work deliberately by asking the students to reflect within the drama on what has happened. For example, we may see three plans enacted in order to choose only one of them: (1) we can rehearse the battle with the monster to check the state of our weapons; (2) we can use a flashback or a flashforward to heighten the choices that we must make; and (3) we can require careful planning exercises using chart paper and markers.

What we want to do with these strategies is elevate the students' feelings and ideas, so that the ensuing drama will be stronger. We are creating an elaborate context for what has happened, not only responding in action but with reflection. Of course, by working in role as teachers, we can offer many more tensions than we could if we were only at the front of the room. Just being able to say, "When I was a young child in this village, I remember something similar happening," adds other directions for the drama to follow.

Role playing

When students role-play, they are propelled into dramatic situations requiring them to think, explore, and interact within a framework of attitudes that may differ from their own. This process helps them gain insight into the motives and feelings of other people within the drama's context. They can be others like themselves, different from themselves, older, younger, more powerful, a different gender, from another place, richer or poorer. They can role-play.

Role playing in groups requires each participant to interact with others, to adjust their in-role responses to the cues of the other players. In doing so, they can learn to work with and respect the ideas of others, while negotiating their own responses. What a powerful tool for teaching students to listen to one another!

It may be useful to assign a role to a particular student if that student repeatedly chooses to play the same sort of role, or if it seems advisable for the student to experience role-playing a type of person unfamiliar to him or her. Degree of involvement with assigned roles may be lower than with roles students choose for themselves, though. It is advisable for teachers to try to strike a balance between the two.

"Playing" in role enables students to join in, to learn by experimenting, to take on different attitudes, and to see how others respond. Role playing is the basis of all drama. When students find the heart of their roles, they will have created drama.

Demonstration: The Emperor's New Clothes—Roles for the Playing

The old story "The Emperor's New Clothes" can provide a basis for many situations that call for role playing. It may be helpful to have the class retell what they remember of the story, and to brainstorm all the roles and incidents that could serve as resources for story drama. The following examples reveal possibilities open to you and your students in exploring a story through drama. (There are numerous other scenarios.)

- You are workers building the special loom on which the marvellous fabric is to be woven. Create the loom with movement and sound. (Groups of 8 to 10)

- You are the swindlers putting on a good show of how diligently and carefully you work at weaving, cutting out, and sewing these garments. (Pairs of students)

- You are the emperor and the two swindlers dressing the emperor for the great procession. The tailors can describe aloud the clothes they are presenting. (Groups of three)

- You are the emperor's entourage (in a tableau or frozen picture) taking part in the procession. (Groups of 10)

- You are the parade marshal planning the procession for the rest of the class, who will create the parade. You describe who will be in it, what the parade route will be, and in what order people will walk in the procession. (Students individually volunteer as parade marshal.)

- You are the emperor's elderly chief counsellor visiting the swindlers. You make excuses for having trouble seeing the material. (Groups of three)

- You are members of a committee representing the citizens of the empire whose emperor spends such huge sums on his clothes. There are a number of building projects, community undertakings, and so forth that need tending to. You go in a group of three to the emperor to present your case on behalf of the empire. Will the emperor and his advisers reluctantly decide to fund one of the projects? (Whole class)

- You, the emperor, have spent the entire empire's treasury on clothes for yourself. Now you must go to the bank for a loan. You must secretly try to convince the bank president that you will be a good credit risk. The bank president is a "shrewd" operator. (Pairs of students)

- You are the emperor's garment workers, and you are exhausted from trying to make all the new clothes the emperor has ordered. You complain as you work. Finally, you decide to go on strike. (Whole class)

- You are the emperor holding a press conference some time after the incident with the swindlers. Reporters still have questions about what happened, but they must be careful in asking them so as not to provoke your anger. You enlist the aid of your chief counsellor in answering the questions. (Whole class)

Strategies for Building a Character

The following two books contain helpful and wide-ranging descriptions of the conventions that we can use to build drama with students:

Structuring Drama Work: A Handbook of Available Forms in Theatre and Drama, Second edition, by Jonothan Neelands and Tony Goode

With Drama in Mind: Real Learning in Imagined Worlds by Patrice Baldwin

Jonothan Neelands and Tony Goode note that the experience of drama requires teachers to use forms and structures that engage both the intellect and the emotions in making and representing collaborative meaning. In their book, *Structuring Drama Work*, they have collected and described dozens of conventions that can be used in planning and implementing a drama lesson, or in developing a drama unit. Throughout this book, you will meet some of these conventions, along with strategies and techniques to support you in constructing drama with your students. As you work in drama, you will discover other modes of representing meaning, and your repertoire of ideas for containing and shaping the work will expand and become refined.

Role on the Wall: Use a life-size outline of a human figure as a cut-out or drawing as the basis for recording the qualities of characters in the drama. The students can read or add statements inside and outside the figure to record and represent a collective understanding of the character's life and attitudes as it develops through the drama. The figure can be talked about, walked around, used within the action of the drama, or used as the basis for an improvised scene.

A Day in the Life: The class creates a sequence of improvised scenes built around 24 hours in the life of the main character of the drama resource. Groups can prepare scenes revealing the incidents in the character's life that help explain the inner conflicts that determined the character's actions and the circumstances. The scenes are then shared in a chronological order, and afterwards, students can revise their scenes from the information gleaned from seeing the entire day's events.

Circle of Life: Aspects of a character's life are represented in four sections of a circle on a large sheet of paper: (1) Home, (2) Family, (3) Play, and (4) Day. Four groups brainstorm the incidents and information about each of the categories that represent the character's life, building up a composite picture from the minimal information offered in the resource. These descriptions can form the basis for the improvisation around the story. Each group works with a different section and creates a brief improvised scene that illustrates the life of the character, using the information that they had created within the drama.

Collective Character: The entire class works together to represent the nature of one character. As the students take turns in speaking the thoughts and words of the character, the character's nature will alter, and students will begin to understand the composite picture they are creating.

Objects of Character: Items can be brought in (or drawn) to flesh out the character in the drama. The objects or possessions can raise questions for the group who will be interpreting how they fit into the character's life. The teacher can provide the items, or the students can present them as artifacts necessary to the building of the drama.

Demonstration: The Red Lion—Exploring Stories of Power

Another powerful story by Diane Wolkstein is *The Magic Orange Tree.*

The Red Lion is a picture book by Diane Wolkstein, and in a demonstration lesson with eight-year-olds and a group of teachers, I chose the role of a prince who was not supposed to speak to villagers. This limitation meant that the students in role as my subjects had to go back and forth to the villagers, played by the adults. Their task was to convince the villagers that I should not have to follow a law about killing a red lion in order to gain the power of a king. This concept was taken from the story directly.

During the first lesson, the students took part in a discussion on how to persuade the villagers that the prince should be allowed to do what he believed and not follow tradition. In pairs, the students as ambassadors then went off to the villagers, who were convinced that the red lion must be killed in the traditional way. The adults as villagers wanted to know why the prince was afraid and what he intended to do to gain power; they then explained that the prince must follow the rules of the land.

Before we next met as a drama class, I prepared some artifacts to support the work. In role as the prince, I called my ambassadors together in order to hear about any problems they might have considered with the villagers. I issued a special badge of honor to each ambassador and through this symbol, the power of the role was heightened. Each student was also presented with a scroll to carry. The scroll partially read, " . . . kill the lion within." As prince, I told my ambassadors they were to explain what this meant to the villagers and at our next meeting, report any questions and doubts the villagers expressed.

Finally, in preparation for their journeys, I asked the students to lie on their backs, close their eyes, and listen. I narrated the story of how a mountain was climbed, and deep within a cave the scroll with this message was discovered. The meaning of the scroll's message, which was addressed to whoever was in charge, caused confusion among the students, but through questioning and discussion, I was able to explore the concept of good versus bad leadership, as well as the ideas of loyalty, bravery, and honesty.

One group of villagers asked if the prince had ever hated or been jealous of anyone. A student role-playing an ambassador explained that these emotions and others like them were the lion within: in order to use power for good, one must destroy the evil or flaws in one's character. Although this concept may have been difficult for the students to comprehend, what is significant is that through the drama, they could stretch their intellects and strive for something slightly beyond their grasp. We had come a long way from killing a lion.

An alternative solution: In another class where the scroll was not employed, the students decided to draft a letter to take to the villagers to explain the prince's refusal to fight a lion. They devised an elaborate scheme involving magic, chanting, and the creation of a surrogate prince who was brought forth from a dream along with a surrogate lion. The wrestling of the lion and the prince, in slow motion, was a powerful moment in the lives of those students, and somehow the demand for blood was satisfied by the use of the dream. And in truth, the lion in their story remained alive and the prince was not forced to kill it.

Reflection

I want these types of stories, filled with power, where the ideas surge up from beneath the words. The books I use over and over are full of caves and shadows, subterranean tunnels, springs that bubble up in odd places, people who are never just what they seem, who trigger in us suspicion or surprise or sadness. I need stories that won't let go, that drag into their midst students who had no intention of entering, students who suddenly grasp the challenge, who at the very least try to escape from the red lion.

These are my stories, ultimately, my dramas. And the tales that the students create lie between the pages of my books, waiting for the next reading, revealing the imprint of the previous class every time I read the author's words to a new group.

Drama Games

See *Games for Everyone: Explore the Dynamics of Movement, Communication, Problem Solving and Drama*, one of my earlier titles, for more detail.

Games present opportunities for drama. For example, the tribe can chant while sitting in a circle, with the sound getting louder as the hunter nears the hunted. The tribe can drum on the floor to accompany the movements of the players, or use rattles or tambourines. The players can wear masks or makeup, or you can change the lighting or use a prop. The words of a game can become the chant the players use to build their drama.

Games can provide students with opportunities to role-play in social situations and to explore unfamiliar relationships. They give them a means of practising on their own and within their own social contexts patterns that will be important in their adult lives. They formalize human interaction processes. As in drama, the players are constantly reversing roles: chasing, being chased, leading, following, shouting, listening, opening the way for understanding social actions and counteractions.

In the drama games that follow, the students are involved and participating with voice and movement.

Monster's Choice: The students form groups of four. Each group has a monster ("it"), which designates who will be the "prey." The three non-monsters join hands and face into the centre of the circle. The monster is outside the circle. When a signal is given, the monster tries to see how many times the "prey" can be tagged while the other players try to prevent it. The monster is not allowed to reach into or across the circle. The leader calls "freeze" to stop the action. The remaining two players become the monster and the prey, and the leader begins play again. For the third round, the original monster and prey switch roles, and so on.

The Rattlers: The students form a circle around two players. These two are both blindfolded and each is given a rattle (tin cans and pebbles make good ones). One (the pursuer) is going to try to tag the other (the quarry). The rattlers enter the "snake pit," and the game begins.

To get a fix on each other's position, rattlers may shake their rattles at any time, with the second rattler immediately responding by shaking hers. However, the pursuer is allowed to initiate only five shakes to locate the quarry, while the pursued can rattle away as much as she dares.

While making sure that neither of the rattlers wanders out of the snake pit, the other players also participate by helping the pursuer keep count of his shakes and cheering and shouting things charming to snakes. To make the game even more interesting, and to keep the other players from feeling like spectators, the teacher can encourage the onlookers to move around, thereby changing the size and shape of the snake pit.

Mirrors: The students operate in pairs, facing each other. One is the mirror; the other is the initiator of the movement. (It is best to have them start slowly with something simple like an isolated arm, hand, or leg movement.) The student who is the mirror imitates the partner's movement as exactly as possible. The students switch roles, so each can be both mirror and initiator. It is best to begin with abstract movements at first, rather than specific activities like, for example, combing hair.

Then the activity is done by two, three, or four pairs, with each mirror person copying the person opposite—the building up of group size should be gradual. In a group mirror, students focus on being aware both of who their partners are and of what the whole group is doing. It is difficult to do this because the whole group must behave in unison.

The mirror people may distort the initiators' movements, as in a fun house at a carnival. The person who is the mirror chooses the type of distortion (making the movement small, big, wide, narrow). The mirror person may experiment with delayed action, so that there is a perceptible pause between the initiator's movement and the reflection of it.

Photocopying: Students operate in groups of three. Student A closes his or her eyes and keeps them closed. Student B assumes any physical shape she or he wishes. Student C gives Student A directions that will permit Student A to become a physical copy of Student B. Student C uses oral instructions only; no physical assistance is permitted.

Moulding Statues: The students work in pairs. One person is the "clay" and starts in a neutral position, such as standing or squatting. The other person, the "sculptor," moulds the "clay" into the shape desired. The sculptor may use sounds and movements, but not words or direct physical contact. When the statue is finished and the position memorized, the students reverse roles.

Joining In: In this activity for student pairs, one person starts to lift an imaginary object; then, a partner joins in to help lift and put it down, following mimed cues received from the initiator of the action. The activity continues with the partners changing the objects they are carrying. The object can be light, heavy, small, large, gooey, smelly, expensive, fragile, dangerous, and so on.

Sound Exploration: Each student selects a location and writes down a list of all of the sounds he or she can hear at this location. The students re-create what they have heard, using words, sounds, and musical instruments to create a soundscape. These sounds may be tape-recorded. Some examples of popular soundscape themes are a playground, a gas station, and a factory. In one instance, a Grade 5 class created soundscapes of a haunted house on Hallowe'en.

Dead One, Arise: Variations of this game are found in Sicily and Germany. Choose one person to lie on the ground and be entirely covered with a blanket, sheet, or pile of jackets. The rest of the group walks around the body calling solemnly, "Dead one, arise! Dead one, arise! Dead one, arise!" No one touches the body, and everyone pretends not to look at it. Then, when least expected, the "dead" person answers the call, rushing at those who have done the "resurrecting." The goal is to touch one of the chanters and make that person the dead one.

- When a victim is caught, he or she joins the "dead" body. Continue until everyone has done so.

- Add music, and perform the game in slow motion.

- Create a story about the dead person—who the person is, how he or she died. Add a ritual to the dramatization in order to indicate that this ceremony is hundreds of years old.

- Extend the story: what happens after the dead person arises?

How a game can lead into drama

Games can often be a preliminary activity for a dramatic situation. This example, Knights and Dragons, demonstrates how a game can be developed into drama; it is possible, though, to do the drama activity without the game.

The game—Catch the dragon's tail: One person is assigned to be a dragon and wears a tail (a piece of material or a scarf sticking out from the back of his or her clothes). Two people try to catch the tail as the dragon runs around the room. When the tail is caught by someone, that person becomes "it."

An extension is for students to make a whole dragon. They line up and join together, each holding on to the waist of the person in front. The line cannot be broken or detached. The scarf becomes the dragon's "tail." The head must try to catch the tail; the "tail" is always trying to escape the head.

Scene I—The dragon problem: The students are told that a dragon has been terrorizing a king's people. They must do something about it. The teacher in role as king says, "I am going to call upon my knights to devise a plan to stop the dragon. I have called you because I know you are heroic knights. I want you to tell me what heroic deed you have done to be on my council." The students respond in role.

The king then tells the students as knights that they each have one magical item or power in order to go out on this mission. Each student explains what the item or power is, how it works, and how it will help slay the dragon.

Scene II—Meeting with the villagers: Then the roles are changed. The students are now villagers and the teacher, in role as the king, says, "I want to meet with the villagers to get a better description of the dragon. What harm has been done? What trouble has the dragon caused you and your community?" In a series of tableaux, the students as villagers then create scenes that show how the dragon attacked or upset the village. These tableaux are shown to the king to demonstrate the problem of the dragon in the kingdom.

Scene III—Return of the knights: The king calls back the knights. In slow motion, students as knights show how they would slay the dragon, using their magical properties. The knights, in groups of three, report to the king how the dragon was destroyed. They try to convince the king that there will be no more trouble and explain the steps taken to destroy the dragon.

Story Tableaux

Story tableaux are frozen pictures, or still images, created in response to a theme, situation, or story. They can crystallize complex or conflicting moments in the drama, allowing students to focus on one significant moment. Participants are often able to interpret or read more into this form of controlled expression. In addition, they learn to contribute to a group effort and gain experience in telling stories and in presenting situations from different points of view.

Here are a few variations on how to approach tableaux:

- *Talking images:* Each member of the frozen picture speaks one line and makes one movement, and as each one takes a turn, those in the picture and those watching gain insight into the issue being presented in the still image.

- *Sculpted images:* A student may mould or sculpt an already existing image to represent individual ideas about the drama being explored, for example: two sides of an issue or the unknown dreams of a character. The student gently moves tableau members into the required positions.

- *Images in series:* Working with a familiar story, a group of four, five, or six students can create two or three images that depict events in the story. Once members identify the high points in the story, they create the series of tableaux. Making smooth transitions from one tableau to the next is important. The groups melt from one tableau to the next as a signal is given. They might also create tableaux based on conflicts, characters, and events "outside" the original story (e.g., a tableau of something that happens just before the story begins or 10 years after the story ends).

- *Mass tableaux:* Students listen to a piece of music, paying attention to the images it suggests to them. The music is played a second time, and any student may go to the centre of the room and assume a position suggested by the music. One by one, the remaining students join the student in the centre to develop a mass tableau. It may be necessary to play the music several times to give everyone time to join in.

- *A prism of images:* A single moment can be represented visually in different ways; for example, the many different gifts given to the king.

- *A pause in the action:* A still image in a drama can be brought to life through improvisation and then frozen again as in a paused video frame.

Demonstration: The Dream Eater—Making Still Images

"The Dream Eater," which is retold in blackline master format, is an excellent source of tableau work. Working in groups of five, students create tableaux of the dreams that disturb the sleep of various characters. When each group has developed its image, the class can observe the tableaux one at a time, until all have been seen.

The Dream Eater

Yukio had a recurring dream each night that he was being chased by a three-headed dream demon riding upon a dragon with 20 eyes. Yukio awoke from his sleep each time the demon was about to devour him. He went to his family for help, but each member that Yukio confronted claimed to have had dreams worse than his.

His father had not slept because he had dreamt that, instead of rice, he had planted bamboo shoots. Without any rice to harvest in the fall, everyone would go hungry, and all because of his foolishness.

Yukio's mother had not slept for three nights. She too had had a terrible dream. In hers, the winter snow turned everything to ice.

Yukio's grandfather had dreamt he was a golden fish swimming in a silver sea. In his dream, he was caught in a fisherman's net and was unable to free himself from the net no matter how he struggled.

Danjuro, the old samurai, told Yukio of his dream that the village was being attacked by fierce bandits riding horses and shooting arrows of fire. Danjuro, in his dream, had only a sword of bamboo with which to fight.

Yukio's father, mother, and grandfather, and the samurai Danjuro sent Yukio away, saying, "It is the time of dreams, and nothing can be done." Yukio found a place by the river to sit and be alone to sleep.

Yukio was awakened by a noise made by the strangest of creatures that, while drinking from the river, had fallen head first into the water. "Help," the creature cried out again and again.

Yukio found a strong vine, which he threw out over the river to rescue the creature. "I owe you my life," the creature said.

The creature explained that he was a baku. A baku eats dreams and nightmares. To a baku, a bad dream is delicious!

The baku asked the young boy for help to satisfy his great hunger. Yukio gladly led the baku to the village. There the baku ate Danjuro's dream of bandits, the grandfather's dream of being caught in a fisherman's net, the mother's dream of a harsh winter, and the father's dream of planting bamboo shoots. They now had pleasant dreams, for the baku had devoured their nightmares.

And when Yukio's dream of demons and dragons came to him, the baku ate every morsel of the nightmare!

Yukio then dreamed of yellow butterflies tanning him on a hot summer's day.

The baku, filled with the bad dreams of the villagers, lay contented.

Movement and Dance in Drama

Movement in drama offers students an opportunity to explore and express thoughts and feelings through physical action. It can serve to increase the student's willingness to get involved in the drama and to encourage interaction with other members of the group. Further, by allowing the students to work creatively and spontaneously, it can enhance the aesthetic learning experience.

Dance drama is movement with the interpretation of a piece of music, a series of sounds, a story, or an emotional theme as its objective. The patterns and rhythms of dance blend with the conflict of the drama, so that the action and feeling of a story are conveyed through movement. Dance drama emphasizes expression rather than form. It can be simple, with each student creating a story independently; or more complex, with groups of students "telling" a story through stylized movement. Dance drama can be supported by music, sound exploration, an accompanying text (either read or narrated), a chant, or costume pieces, such as masks or capes.

Through movement in drama, students develop concentration and physical control; they extend and improve their kinesthetic sense and spatial awareness. The good "group feeling" generated by movement activities promotes the trust in and sensitivity to others required for drama growth.

Movement in drama can be used in these ways:

- as a warm-up or lead-in activity for a lesson

- as a mood setter at the start or finish of a lesson

- within the context of the drama situation

- as a basis or framework on which to build the drama

Moving to music

Building an environment: The students move freely around the room to a piece of selected music. As they move, the teacher tells them they are in a series of different environments and situations: for example, deep snow, sinking sand, a small tunnel, a huge spider web, a dark cave. They adjust their movements accordingly. The students should be given adequate time to explore each new situation, using the whole body.

Telling stories: Music that is strong in evoking images and that offers changes in mood, pace, and rhythm should be selected for this activity. The students find comfortable positions on the floor, close their eyes, and listen to the music. If they have previously taken part in a strenuous physical activity, they will find it easier to relax. After listening to the music, they briefly discuss the images they saw while listening. They then form groups of four, and each student in the group describes the story he or she imagined. The group chooses one student's story, or parts of each student's story and, through movement only, tells the story. To encourage slow, graceful movement, it is advisable to play the music throughout the activity and to suggest to the students that the story is a dream.

Mime

Mime is dramatic action that depends on gesture and movement rather than on words. It stresses exploration of ideas without dialogue. Its simplicity permits the emergence of thoughts and emotions that are sometimes difficult to convey in words. As a result, mime encourages free and spontaneous expression with the students. They act and respond to what they see, hear, taste, and touch. Mime lends itself equally well to activities for large or small groups, students working in pairs, or students working independently. The use of mime in drama moves students into an "action" mode rather than a "talking" mode, and can reveal specifics about the drama that could go unnoticed.

Mime games can introduce students to the "as if" way of working:

Passing the Object: Students sitting in a circle are asked by the teacher to imagine that there is a sink in front of them. They wash their hands. They hold up their hands and think about how they feel. (Often hands feel wet or soapy.) Then, an imaginary object is passed around the circle. If the students want to change the object, they are free to do so, indicating, with mime only, what the new object is.

The Wounded Bird: The students sit in a circle. The teacher folds a piece of exercise paper, then says: "We are going to imagine that this is a wounded bird. We will pass it around the circle, and each of you will treat it as such. Let's see who helps make the bird seem real for us." When the bird returns to the teacher, she takes it gently and then unfolds the paper with a quick gesture.

Narration and mime

Narration and mime can be used within the drama to build mood, to calm students down, or to focus the drama. The students may enact the narrative together, each making a personal response. Or, the students may work in pairs or small groups. The teacher can narrate students through a series of mime activities, building in opportunities for individual choices or decisions.

This activity works well with beginning groups and as a warm-up for experienced groups. Selections may be created to complement a particular curriculum (e.g., science) or chosen and adapted from stories. The selections may be edited to stress the physical action, and dialogue may be added by the students as they extend the mime into drama.

Rituals

A ritual is a series of actions or activities done in exactly the same way every time they are performed. In many societies, rituals are believed to have special power and the way in which they are performed takes on great symbolic significance. For example, some early clans or tribes used magic, dancing, masks, or costumes to enhance the power of a ritual. All these aspects would help make the ritual unique.

The rituals of early societies were very important in these peoples' lives. They brought individuals together, focusing all their thoughts and energy on one activity. Everyone worked towards the same goal. In this way, ritual taught a people what was expected of them, which allowed the group to maintain control and structure. As well, through ritual, the knowledge and beliefs of the society were passed on to future generations. The group experience took over and an understanding shared by all was created.

In a ritual, members of a society enact their hopes and fears. Some societies believed that ritual would influence nature and the gods. For example, before a bear hunt, warriors might act out the killing of the bear, with one hunter being the bear and other hunters the attackers. The people felt that this would make the gods sympathetic to their cause and help in the killing of a bear.

Ritual is also very important to students of drama. For one thing, early primitive rituals were the beginning of formal theatre: the duties of the priest and other participants in the ritual gradually became roles taken on by actors; the other members of the group went from being worshippers to audience members. As well, for students of drama, rituals offer a tremendous source of material for creative work. Students can create their own rituals and use these as part of a drama they are creating, or as the beginning or ending of the drama.

Demonstration: The Bear Hunt—Ritual Making

Primitive men have searched in vain for food for the hungry tribe. It is time for another approach. A medicine man places a bear's head over the head of a hunter. The hunter growls, uses his hands as though they are paws, and lumbers about. He has become the bear. The other men imitate him, prowl and dance around him, and "hunt" him. They pretend to thrust spears into the bear, which then falls to the ground. The medicine man pretends to cut off the head. With a shout, the head is speared and held high. The medicine man leads the hunters in a dance of triumph. The dancers believe that they have made such strong magic during the dance that they will more easily find food.

In two or three groups (depending upon the size of the class), prepare the ritual of the bear hunt. The ritual should begin slowly and gather momentum as the hunters move in to "kill" the bear. Here are some suggested elements to consider in preparing the drama.

- How will you communicate the feeling of extreme hunger?

- How will you represent the searching of food?

- Will the bear be represented by a single person, a pair, a small group?

- How will the bear move? What will it sound like?

- How will the medicine man be portrayed?

- What are some other roles that the participants could take?

- Will there be standing? crouching? leaping? prowling?

- Will there be dancing?

- Will you imitate the bear's actions?

- How will the space be used? A circle? A line?

- How will the hunters approach the bear? close in on it? capture it?

- Will you use a drum or any other instrument to beat a rhythm?

- Will any props, costumes, or makeup be used to enhance the ritual?

- Can you create masks for the ceremony?

- How can you create the fierceness and bravery of the hunters?

- What nonverbal sounds will you use? Grunts? Growls? Moans? Humming?

- Will you use any words?

- Will there be places of silence? stillness?

- Will the ritual include the killing of the bear? If so, how will it be handled?

- Will there be some group work that will then be made part of the whole in presenting the ritual?

- How will you end? Quietly? With a yell? Fading out? Building up? With music or chant?

Ways of Working in Drama

Be sure to check out *Beginning Drama 11–14* by Jonothan Neelands.

Drama should involve as many students as possible. Generally, it is best if all the students work with you at the same time in setting up the drama frame and in establishing how the drama can proceed. All variations in grouping are necessary for drama to develop: the student alone, the small group, the whole class.

Independent work

Sometimes, the students will work independently without interacting with others. This provides an opportunity for deepening concentration, allows privacy for individual exploration, and minimizes distractions. The class works as a single unit, but with each individual functioning as a part of the whole. (*Each of you is creating a statue for the courtyard of the medieval church. As I walk among you and tap you on the shoulder, show me what you have chosen to create and quietly describe your work to me.*)

Some students seem to demand immediate and continuous involvement and need to be pressed into deeper achievement; others must be persuaded to participate. We must continually accept their efforts and encourage them to extend their involvement. The meanings that will accrue in a student's life grow from personal involvement and experience.

Group work

Sometimes, the students will work in pairs or in small groups, stimulating each other's thinking and lending support to other members of the group. Each student needs to work with a variety of partners, and the tasks can be carefully designed. There need be little sharing, but groups can demonstrate or depict some of their findings, so that there is a sense of community rather than competition. (*The group can now share with us their plans for getting past the guards at the moat.*)

Working in small groups is an excellent way of developing drama skills. It lets all students be part of the group process, sharing ideas and feelings, perhaps changing their opinions or getting other people to change theirs, and finally reaching an agreement. The learning that happens in drama most often takes place during group exploration, and small groups can cover more ground than large groups can.

In a small-group improvisation, three to five people should take part. This group size allows all of the students to participate and to get to know one another's strengths. Students should also work with different people at different times, so that they gain the experience of building their roles in different contexts. As you move from group to group, you may sometimes encounter leadership difficulties about such issues as who decides a course of action or plays which role. Remember that each individual must feel part of the group, so by negotiating with the members of each group, you can find ways for all of them to become part of the dramatic action.

There are ways to strengthen the group work. You can move about the room, questioning groups, challenging ideas, promoting deeper thought, communicating ideas between groups, resetting a problem, defining a focus. You may structure the task-centred problem—solving in pairs or in small groups, encouraging student-to-student interaction. While working with the students in various groups, you can play a different role with each group.

I have learned, though, that it is important to call the groups back together to check on what has been happening. "What discussion has your group had?" "Did everyone agree?" "What caused your group to think this way?" "Do you agree with what the other groups have said?" The students must feel that what occurred during the group time was important to them personally and to the drama activity as a whole.

Drama is a corporate act. It involves the negotiation of meaning between individuals with different views of what is being worked on in the drama. The teacher assists the class, building a contract where all the participants are making conscious and deliberate decisions in the safety of fictional role. The greatest growth in the students' understanding of thoughts and feelings of people in the drama situation occurs when the whole class is working together, and where small-group work helps deepen the drama for that experience.

Small groups contributing to whole-class drama

There are many good reasons for wanting to share a group's work. If each group's work is part of a theme that the whole class is exploring, it helps to see the interpretation that others have developed on the same topic. Or, groups may be exploring a single situation from different viewpoints. (For example: One group might show a situation from a parent's point of view, another group from a teenager's point of view, and another from the peer group's point of view.) You may wish, in presenting a scene, to use the rest of the class in role. For example, they can all be at a parent–teacher event.

The freedom to explore a situation in drama fully, without the pressure of being watched, can lead eventually to a presentation, but it is while they are exploring the drama and interacting with each other that most learning takes place. It is the shared responsibility of the role players to develop the drama. All players should be prepared to adjust their actions in order to help move the drama along in a mutually satisfactory way. By listening and responding to the others in the group, members can create the drama moment to moment, responding spontaneously to the challenges presented. Once a group has understood its own improvised drama, then perhaps the drama can be polished and reworked for another group to watch.

There are so many ways to let group work play a part in the growth of whole-class drama:

- Each group may report back to the whole class in role (or choose a spokesperson, such as an elder).

- Each group may show a moment of the learning that they arrived at, in tableau or in depicting a special incident; several groups may volunteer to demonstrate some aspect of their learning.

- The groups may re-create an incident which occurred in the drama experience.

- The individuals, in a circle, may express in role their feelings about the group's work.

- The teacher may freeze a point in the action of each group (it may not be beneficial to show all the work of each group to one another).

- As structured by the teacher, the work that went on in groups can be the basis for the next part of the drama lesson; the group work may become a play within the larger context of the whole-class drama experience, a play within a play.

- Perhaps the most important time for sharing the work is when it might serve as the beginning of a drama that the whole class can then explore.

Whole-class work

The whole class can take part in a single improvisational workshop, acting as a drama ensemble. Events such as meetings, assemblies, inquiries, and protests allow the whole class to participate in this way, contributing in and out of role. New kinds of learning may happen, since all the students may be asking questions, sharing ideas, negotiating with one another, and making choices and decisions; however, there will be much

The way in which the group works together determines the quality of the work that the group does. Whether students are working with a partner, a small group, or the whole class, the behavior of each individual affects the group. Drama demands co-operation in order that a single focus can be created.

more to listen and respond to, and, of course, there will be much more feedback to explore. By exploring and expanding the ideas and suggestions, the class can build the drama co-operatively into a playmaking event.

Even in a whole-class improvisation, students will need to work in pairs or in small groups from time to time in order to complete specific tasks. For example:

- There may be a need to explore several sides to a particular issue.

- The class may want to stop the drama and explore various interpretations of the problem.

- Each pair or small group can present its idea, and the class can choose one as the most suitable with which to continue.

- The whole group might decide to include the thoughts of several small groups and redirect the drama.

- There may be times when you, as the teacher, need to work out of role to negotiate problems that have arisen, and then continue the drama when the members have accepted the compromise.

- There may also be times when the disagreement between the groups is a more interesting idea for the drama than finding a single solution.

The large number of participants means that you, as the teacher, need to act as a moderator or director, and guide the drama along. In order to focus and extend student ideas, you can present other options to the class. At times, you may even assume a role in the drama, questioning, asking for clarification, helping students make decisions. By working inside the drama, you help the class in building powerful drama. The many participants can add to the event's excitement and tension. This type of ensemble work has group dynamics as its "mind" and theatre as its "heart."

Uniting Heart and Mind

My colleague and friend Gano Haine uses tension as a way of deepening, enriching, and extending the drama. In a medieval drama, children in Grade 5 were trying to get their true king returned to them. They decided to be bird trainers, sending messages by carrier pigeon to the imprisoned king. Right away, through her questioning, her taking on role, her setting the specifics to be explored by partners, groups, and the whole class, Gano asked us about our preparations for the pigeons to fly. She wanted to know who was in charge of tagging the pigeons, who would sweep the coop, who would feed the birds. She had each of us hold an imaginary pigeon, to check its wings, to make sure that it would be able to fly with the message. As a village, we had to test the pigeons' abilities to see which one would be given the message—one and only one. We fed and cared for them and made them real. Finally, Gano picked one imaginary pigeon feather from the floor, put it between the pages of her book and said, "In this feather is the freedom of our kingdom."

This chapter surveys the different strategies, conventions, and techniques that we, as drama educators, find useful in developing drama experiences with our students. Incorporating a variety of them in our lessons allows us to achieve a range of goals. By our choice of tools, we can draw a class's attention to an aspect of the work they had not noticed. With a technique that offers and demands a different way of responding, we can alter the dynamic of the dramatic interaction by changing the mode of representing ideas or shifting the nature of the emotional engagement. With a strategy that moves them to a different viewpoint, an altered perception, we can support or challenge the students' ideas. By our choice of a convention, we can cause drama participants to make a stronger emotional response, deepening the significance of the issues being explored.

As we grow in our knowledge of conventions, strategies, and techniques useful in our drama practice, we are more able to build drama experiences that are multi-layered, that move far beyond stereotypical responses to the events being interpreted and represented. In each instance, we can choose the strategies that strengthen and enhance the particular event being explored through drama. We can offer ourselves and our students alternative ways of being within the drama.

Chapter 4: Finding Dramatic Ways for Students to Retell Stories

Children have many stories to tell. The issue is: Will they tell them to you?

Harold Rosen

I have come to realize that in my work I retell, narrate, summarize, and recount frequently; in other words, tell stories. Drama has allowed me the strength in role to tell the stories I have read aloud for years, encapsulating what has gone before the drama, as I recount the story that the village hands down to its young, or when I adopt a role in an attempt to deepen or redirect the drama work. I can use story to slow down the actions, reminding the students of what has gone on or preparing them for what may come next. Jonothan Neelands calls these "stories in action," developed from the responses of the group and the needs of the drama. We incorporate necessary details, elevate language, present a serious focus full of subtextual significance, and relate personal anecdotes from our own lives.

See *Drama, Narrative and Moral Education: Exploring Traditional Tales in the Primary Years* by Joe Winston for more on this subject.

When students tell stories, they gain time to consider the dramatic activity they have been engaged in building. Rather than show their thoughts, they can tell them within the structure of story, in pairs, in small groups, or as a large gathering. Brief narratives told by students in role can include gossip, rumor, wisdom, reports, observations, customs, culture, rules, codes, and metaphors. They can be told informally in small settings or formally as an attempt to persuade the whole group of a particular point of view. Either way, they help students come to an understanding of what a storyteller needs to achieve his or her purpose—an invaluable lesson in creating drama experiences for students.

Story Sources

In *Story Works* by David Booth and Bob Barton, Bob Barton shares his deep understanding of storytelling as a force for drama teaching.

When I am asked where I find my sources for drama, I can only reply, "From everywhere." My friend Bob Barton is a consummate storyteller, and I admire his ability to act as a medium for the hundreds of stories he has come to know, as he says, by heart rather than by memory. In my own work, though, I use print sources as often as possible because I also am a literacy and literature teacher. And, of course, among thousands of books for young people, some speak to me louder than others as sources for dramatic exploration.

In particular, the picture book is an ingenious and all-encompassing source: so much can be discovered and rediscovered by the children as they explore both the language and the pictures. It's a unique medium. The words are written to be spoken and the pictures are intended to broaden and complement so that the settings for these books are often

Novels written as poems offer us dozens of powerful monologues to build our drama lessons around. Students can read aloud examples of quality writing, and then the class can create their own story dramas. Look for these titles:

Poems from Homeroom: A Writer's Place to Start
  by Kathi Appelt
Love That Dog
  by Sharon Creech
Heartbeat
  by Sharon Creech
Keesha's House
  by Helen Frost
Out of the Dust
  by Karen Hesse
Aleutian Sparrow
  by Karen Hesse
17: A Novel in Prose Poems
  by Liz Rosenberg
Becoming Joe DiMaggio
  by Maria Testa
Girl Coming in for a Landing: A Novel in Poems
  by April Halprin Wayland

Storyteller Bob Barton says, "Instead of planning in a vacuum, we start with a book that we know well and we find the power of drama within it."

rare and usually dramatic. The age of the children I work with seems irrelevant because the picture book appeals to everyone, especially to today's visually oriented television viewers. The well-chosen picture book embodies those qualities of story and image that draw the children's own experiences to the page; it lets them see and hear new meanings as they negotiate between their own world and the world of the author/illustrator. Picture books open up opportunities for discussion and deepen understanding as the pictures catch the eye, supported by the text and the imagination. The picture book can be the experience; drama can help make sense of that experience.

Folktales also allow me to use their "bones" as the beginnings of my drama work. If you think of them as preserved and performed by generations of storytellers, then they speak to the child in all of us, symbolizing deep feelings and using fantastic figures and events. No matter how ancient a story is, it's not archaeological remains, but a living tale that we can examine, offering glimpses of a particular time or a particular culture. These stories have acquired significance as they passed through time. Our stories of today are built on stories of the past.

Even the novel can be a useful source. It can allow us to see just what story can offer us in building drama. Although it is too long and complicated to be dramatized, the novel lets us take from it themes, characters, and incidents that will act as supportive frameworks for drama work.

Students as Storytellers

Storytelling can enrich and extend students' personal hoard of words, ideas, stories, songs, and concepts, and deepen their understanding and appreciation of literature. Storytelling increases their mastery of language by showing them that words can be manipulated into new meanings. It helps them actively internalize language structures and styles, and develops the ability to turn narration into dialogue and dialogue into narration. It encourages role playing, which, in turn, gives students valuable practice in shifting their point of view and in experimenting with different styles of language and a variety of voices:

- Storytelling is one of the first ways we develop an awareness of others and of ourselves as spectators. As children, we liked having stories read or told aloud to us. We also enjoyed taking on the role of storyteller, telling our favorite stories to others. In drama, storytelling is one way of communicating with an audience, and it is a technique that every audience can identify with.

- Students can tell stories in a circle, with a partner, through mime and tableau, chorally, or as narration for mime. They can improvise from the story, change the story, or find the new stories within the story.

- Storytelling can provide the initial starting point for the drama; it can reveal an unexplained idea in even a well-known story; it can focus details; it can be a review of what has already taken place; or it can be a way of building reflection in role.

- The students can retell stories they have heard, develop themes within that story, or build new stories.

- Using picture books without text, students can describe in their own words what they see happening, sometimes supplying the characters with what they feel is appropriate dialogue. Showing students unusual and exciting pictures may also promote storytelling.

- Students may enjoy playing the different characters as they tell the story. Or students may dramatize a story while it is being told, assuming the parts of different characters (e.g., a witch, a bird, and two lost children).

- As the storyteller spins the tale, the teacher may signal for someone to continue the story, or another student may choose to continue on his or her own at a dramatic pause in the story.

- A "talking stick" is held by each student when it is his or her turn to speak, and is passed on to the next student when the speaker stops (sometimes in mid-phrase).

- In a larger group, the teacher tells an improvised story, pauses every so often, and points to someone in the group to add an appropriate word. "Once upon a time there was a young . . . He walked until suddenly . . . He said . . . "

- One student retells to a partner a story which the teacher told; then, the second student tells the story back to the first student.

- In an exercise in crossed communications, one student begins telling a partner a story. The object for each student is to get to the end of the story without being distracted by the partner. As a variant, the students work in groups of three. Two students tell stories simultaneously and compete for the attention of the third.

- Begin a round-robin storytelling activity by dividing the class into small groups and asking each person in a group to read the same story silently. When students have finished, number them off. On a pre-arranged signal, student 1 from each group begins to retell until the signal sounds. Student 2 takes over, then student 3, and so on (in this way the story is retold with no one person responsible). Students can explore first-person narrations by retelling from various points of view or try multipart narration, where one narrator shapes the tale while others retell from their chosen point of view. Finally, students can get inside the story by exploring a challenging or magical part, creating a chant or rhyme to "help" the characters out of difficulty.

- After a read-aloud, provide each student (or pairs of students) with a long strip of paper. Ask them to draw a series of pictures that retell the story and to include captions, labels, and signs where possible. Picture retelling can be used with a variety of texts, including nursery rhymes, biographies, poems, and chapter books. Students can compare their retellings with those completed by their classmates. Did they choose to illustrate the same events? If not, how did this affect the retelling?

Demonstration: The Tree—Retelling and Passing on Stories

Several years ago, I had the pleasure of listening to Bill Martin Jr. read aloud his story *The Ghost-Eye Tree* to a summer school of teachers. In the story, two children are afraid to walk past the ghost-eye tree in the middle of town because of the stories told about its power. I knew then I had a perfect source for story drama, and I read the story to a Grade 4 class at a demonstration session at a drama conference. The students and I shared personal anecdotes about frightening experiences; the participating teachers retold legends they had created previously to small groups of students, recounting the origins of the stories generated by the ghost-eye tree.

Rumors and incredible stories: Within the context of the ensuing drama, I, in role as a new teacher at the school, listened to the students role-playing students volunteering to tell me the story of the village tree. I questioned each aspect of their stories, causing them to elaborate and extend their legend through my seeming disbelief. When I chose to spend the night at the tree to prove the silliness of their stories, they tried to dissuade me by sharing other incidents that had happened over the years to strengthen the tale of the tree's power; however, I told them I was going to put an end once and for all to the rumors. Out of role, the students discussed their feelings about the events that had occurred in the drama.

A change in role: The next scene was established by my entering the room as the principal, explaining that the teacher had not shown up for work and could not be reached at home. I asked the students for any information they might have about his absence, and none responded. I stopped the drama lesson at this point, told them my version of what I thought this lesson was about, and the class broke into groups in an attempt to explain the teacher's disappearance.

The whole class listened to each group's story, and after some discussion, accepted this as the official record:

> *Mr. Booth went to the tree two years ago and fell and*
> *hit his head. Some people thought he was dead, but*
> *really he has suffered some sort of memory loss.*

Surprisingly, I received a package two years later from a student in that class, explaining how her teacher had saved the subsequent writings of the students and used them inside a new drama with a different class. The storying continued for two years in the school setting, and perhaps extends into their lives even now. I had been the original storyteller, but the students had gained the confidence to take over.

Reflection

This drama work allowed students to tell stories of many kinds: recollections from the drama experiences as told by those who had lived through the fictional situation; personal anecdotes about what happened to the students both inside and outside the drama; personal stories stimulated by and enriched through the drama experience; literary retellings of the story used by the teacher to suggest the drama, retold from the perspective of the participants in role to those who must hear what has happened; collective stories by groups and by the whole class, wherein they revisited or recounted their own experiences drawn from the drama, in parallel to the teacher's story. Storytelling is a meaning-making process within the drama and without, prompting reflective discussion and writing in private journals and in more public venues, such as the classroom newspaper.

Demonstration: Oliver Hyde in Hiding—Trusting the Work

This lesson required some preplanning with a group of 30 teachers in Chicago. That morning, I taught them the words to a chant from *Oliver Hyde's Dishcloth Concert*, the book by Richard Kennedy that we would attempt to build upon:

> Oliver Hyde is a strange old man,
> He sticks his head in a coffee can,
> And hides his face when there's folks about,
> He's outside in, and he's inside out.

Scene I: We were accompanied by a teacher on course, a gifted musician playing several instruments throughout the day, including the kinnor, which King David supposedly played. We began by listening to the musician's songs and relating the images created in our minds by the sounds of the kinnor. Interestingly, the students conjured up ideas from King Arthur, the Bible and what they called "songs from the farms and hills." It was a quick step to the next phase of the work, with groups of four or five students listening to teachers retelling the tall tale from the day before; this time, though, the teachers were asked to dramatize the story in role, painting a picture of the Ozark community that would eventually contain the drama. As well, the teachers in role invited the youngsters to become members of mountain families, using mimed tasks to involve them.

Scene II: We all joined a large circle and sang the Oliver Hyde chant that had been rehearsed earlier, accompanied by the musician, another teacher playing washboard, and free-form folk dancing. Teachers and students were all involved. Next, in groups of five, the teachers and the students created small tableaux, each group making two photographs for a community scrapbook that included Oliver Hyde: one serious picture and one "outtake" from the back of the album. One group at a time viewed the other frozen pictures and discussed their ideas and opinions about the context of each tableau they had seen. When we had all shared our tableaux, Oliver Hyde was removed from each of the photographs (one student per tableau). As narrator, I informed the class that this person, Oliver Hyde, had not been a part of this town for years. He now sat at home with a paper bag over his head, and we didn't know why. Students playing Oliver Hyde were given a paper bag each and sat apart from the class, trying on their masks.

Scene III: The small groups had to decide why Oliver had been in hiding, and then share with the large group the rumors or stories they had created about him. To strengthen their work, as teacher in role, I said to all: "I want Oliver at my wedding. He once saved my life. He will come out tonight for one hour to your homes to speak with you. You must help me convince him to come to the wedding, take the bag off his head, and play his fiddle." The small groups had to decide on a strategy that would convince each student in role as Oliver. This took almost 30 minutes.

Scene IV: Each Oliver met with his small group twice and could respond to their persuasions only by nodding or shaking his head due to the paper bag over the head. After half an hour of intensive questioning, none of the students had yet removed their masks. In role as the bridegroom, I asked each Oliver in turn to come to the wedding. I offered that the bride and I would wear paper bags to match his. I then said to all the students in role as Oliver: "Will you take your mask off, Oliver?" The tension was high as we waited for each student to respond. One by one, each Oliver Hyde made a personal decision, and in this case, all the students took off their bags. In celebration, the whole group danced to live music at the wedding, incorporating the song we had sung at the beginning of the drama. A teacher even performed a clog dance for us, as we clapped along with the music. A student and I, as bride and groom, danced in the circle as the drama closed.

Reflection

I knew the day before that the drama lesson had to follow the genre of musical theatre, as the students felt that to be their mandate for the summer. As teacher, I wanted them to centre their work on the story they were creating, and to use the other arts to strengthen their drama. The musician was a wonder, improvising his tunes to our needs at the moment, underscoring our work and providing counterpoint to our rhythms. The paper bags used as masks were a powerful symbol for our work.

One teacher commented on the advantages of our exercises: "David needed time to choose students to pull out of groups to become Oliver. Tableaux gave this time to him to observe the students." I found that even when Oliver, as an outsider, was removed from a tableau picture, he left a hole in the picture, almost like someone had cut him out.

I must say this was one of my favorite lessons. The moment of everyone dancing around on the floor to the glorious music was a wonderful celebration for the ending of the story, but also of the whole creation process. I finally understood that I should let the work be my focus, not my fear that the students may not be involved or that my deepening ability could harm the drama. Trust the work, and the students will give what they can give, and the teachers will give what they can give.

Storytelling from a Point of View

Many stories are generated by the drama stories drawn from the original sources: stories only suggested by or first hidden in the shadows of the original, stories that evolved as the drama took shape, stories told about the story or the storyteller, stories reflecting and distancing the whole drama experience, and stories from the lives of the students, evoked by the drama. Drama offers us countless characters and situations for narrating the different stories both during and at the close of the drama event.

The storytelling roles that are chosen by the students (or by the teacher) often determine the impact of the storying. They can alter the direction of the drama, increase the tension, deepen the understanding of what has happened, explain a character's motivation, present a conflicting viewpoint, or summarize the drama experience.

Retelling the story from the viewpoint of one of the characters can deepen the drama that has been constructed. Consider the possibilities for storytelling when a student or a teacher adopts one of these roles:

- Reporter: *Here is what I have chosen to tell about.*

- Witness: *I was there and I saw it all.*

- Neighbor: *My neighbor told me all about what happened.*

- Friend: *I need to tell you what happened to my friend.*

- Gossip: *You won't believe what I just heard.*

- Commentator: *This is the news! Today, this story is just in.*

- Leader: *Listen, my people! You must understand what I will tell you.*

- Rebel: *Don't believe a word of this story!*

- Judge: *I seek to uphold the law.*

- Parent: *When I was a child, this story was so important to me.*

- Therapist: *Your problems will be revealed in this story I will tell you.*

- Police officer: *Here is what happened, your honor.*

- Government bureaucrat: *This story is the official word of the government.*

- Social worker: *We must do something about the people in this story.*

- Conscience: *What fills my mind as I tell the story?*

- Alien: *How amusing. This story would not happen in my world.*

- Spokesperson: *I will tell you this story so that we know how to proceed.*

- Patient: *After I tell this story, you will know what happened to me.*

- Inmate: *I tell this story to fill my jail with sunshine even for a moment.*

- Family member: *This story has been passed down in our family.*

- Traitor: *This is not exactly how it happened. Let me tell you.*

- Seer: *I will tell you a story and it will come true.*

- Spirit: *I want to tell you the story. Can you see or hear me?*

- Coach: *Let me help you tell the story.*
- The chosen one: *Only I can relate what has befallen all of us.*
- Robot: *I have recorded what has happened and I will play it back.*
- Artist: *I will transform the event according to my own needs.*

Instruments for Storytelling

We want our students to tell stories, to shape their own life anecdotes, to retell those we have shared in our drama, to add narratives to the improvised work they are creating together, to see storytelling as an important and valuable means of representing both experience and ideas. Something powerful happens when we tell stories in role: we can use the context of the drama event to uncover and unleash our own storying possibilities. As we draw upon the roles that we inhabit, we find ourselves, both students and teachers, able to participate in the art form called storytelling with added emotional power. We can change the syntax, the style, the voice, the mannerisms to fit the role, and the narrative lifts the drama work, giving it a texture that engages the listener-participants and the storyteller. We need to use this powerful instrument more often in our drama making—everyone in the imaginary garden has a story to tell and a right to be heard.

Chapter 5: Choosing Structures for Creating Drama on the Story

A librarian friend first gave me the book *The King's Fountain* 25 years ago, and I have been happily trapped in it ever since. Surely it is the vast possibilities that constantly draw me to it as a source for drama, a story so bare yet so intense that it seems unexplored every time I consider it as a beginning point for learning in role. This book is one of my most important sources for drama teaching, with dozens of lessons for students of all ages, about the feelings engendered in us by the author and the illustrator, and our attempts to give form and voice to those feelings. A simple tale by Lloyd Alexander, illustrated by Ezra Jack Keats, echoing stories of desert tribes and powerful kings, it leaves magical spaces for students to fill in, like a tapestry worn in parts by time; our eyes struggle to find completeness, to grasp the whole picture.

A king wishes to build a fountain "for the splendor of his kingdom and the glory of his name." Doing this would take all of the water from the village at the foot of the palace hill, though, causing suffering and despair to the people. An old man attempts to persuade others to speak to the king, but they all offer excuses, and his daughter suggests that he himself must make the journey up to the palace. Keats paints a rugged terrain, with a great chasm between the man and the king, and the subsequent meeting of the two results in the king not building the fountain.

One Story, Many Paths

That is the story, but as in all folktales, the reader must bring to the text a world of context and understanding, and drama allows us to create a collaborative experiencing of story, creating a single tapestry of group responses to the tale. No two creations will be alike; despite the fact that every creation begins with the same narrative, every group's efforts seem connected, yet separate. After all these years, I have never lost interest in this story, for the very nature of improvised drama means that every experience will follow a different path, dependent upon the context of the group at that time.

I am the storyteller, but in time, in role, students will tell me their story. All of us in the class are necessary to the storymaking, as we engage in filling in between the lines, digging within the words, arguing about textual intent. We build our own story, and in the end it may not resemble *The King's Fountain* in structure, but all the accrued understandings of the tale will be woven into the creation.

These books by Lloyd Alexander are full of contemporary action in a seemingly historic world, and serve as ideal resources for events to explore:

The King's Fountain
The Iron Ring
The Kestrel (Firebird)

The Teaching Challenge

See *The New Dramathemes*, Third edition, by Larry Swartz.

How will I know which road to follow with each group? This is the drama teacher's struggle: listening, watching, setting up situations that will foreshadow the direction of the journey, knowing when to intervene, when to use a particular strategy to open up discussion, to move the students into action, to cause them to pause, to reflect, to rethink, and all this without predetermining the learning, the content, the meat of the lesson. We provide the play dough for them to model, and in drama, we will sculpt together, each attempt affecting all others, the individual finding strength from the group, and the group enriching and extending each individual.

When they have heard the tale, what will the students say? What will they take as their beginning points? What will they reveal about their lives and attitudes? Who will lead and who will support those leaders? What will I as teacher do throughout the lesson to deepen their sensibilities, clarify their inconsistencies, alter their conceptions, frame their learning? So many questions arise from such a brief book: this simple legend compresses many concepts into a brief narrative, and the questions below have been generated by dozens of classes in their attempts to understand the complexities of this archetypal situation. Each question the students ask, every comment they make, all the concerns I raise, give me insight into how I may want to construct the lesson: perhaps a game to open up energy, to initiate ideas, a technique such as creating a tableau to highlight a significant moment.

I am afraid I spend little time in "one-on-one" in drama teaching, for having sensed the power of the group, I want to unleash it so that students can together create a play that, perhaps without audience, will reveal the thrill of theatre, of using improvised dialogue to build our sense of story. As in all teaching, we watch, wait and suggest, letting the connections emerge, the learning develop. We need the hour, the day, the year. Our content will be the beginning, but the lessons will grow on their own, in their own shape and time.

Demonstration: The King's Fountain—Questioning the Story

The following list represents just a fraction of the questions that have arisen after readings of the story to classes of teachers and students. Your students will come up with questions of their own—the list is potentially endless.

- What was the king's name? the old man's? the girl's?

- Why did the king want to build the fountain?

- Why had the village relied upon a single source of water for its very life?

- What were the king's true motives in building this fountain? Is there another way the king could show his glory to the people?

- Where were the king's advisers in all of this?

- How many soldiers did the king have?

- How do you represent visually the trappings of power?

- Why were the wise people afraid to go to the king?

- What was so intimidating about the king that no one would approach him?

- Had an event like the building of the fountain happened in the past?

- What happened in the king's past that made him think that it was appropriate to take away the village's water?

- Why was the old man allowed to stand before the king when he was captured?

- What did the little girl say or do? What was her role in the story? Was it the child's words that changed the king's mind?

- What did the girl say to inspire her father to speak with the king?

Demonstration: Gifts for the King—Reworking the Drama Experience

When one energetic first-grade group worked with the same story, they decided to explore the need for water in our world.

Scene I: Extrapolating from their real-life roles as powerless children to the villagers in the drama, the children opted to take gifts to the king, in an attempt to dissuade him from building the fountain. In small groups with student teacher scribes, they brainstormed suggestions for offerings for the ruler, and then, moving into action drama, they rehearsed how each family would present its tributes. I offered some prompts as tension to help them build their scenes:

- Will everyone go forward to meet the king or will someone be chosen?

- Will you show respect to the king or be angry?

- How will you approach the throne?

- What if each family gives the same gift?

- Shall we watch each other's groups to see how we should behave?

- Do we need any special costumes or objects?

Scene II: After the general hubbub of practice, we were ready to meet the king. Fortunately, I could work inside the learning as teacher in role, focusing the drama, elevating the language, adding tension, clarifying actions, but not predetermining outcomes. I selected to role-play the king, since as a visitor to the classroom, I could play upon my lack of identity, and the students could use their social group as a safety network. How would I use surprise and tension to provoke thoughtful response? That was my constant quest.

By sitting on a chair on top of the teacher's desk, I literally elevated the power of the king and changed the spatial arrangement of the class into a physical relationship between subjects and ruler. I needed to say very little, as my position directed the flow of dialogue. The groups, in turn, made their way up an aisle created by the students and the teachers, a theatrical form to heighten their sense of presentation. They mimed presenting such tributes as these—a cloak lined with rubies and diamonds, a throne of gold and silver, a crown of emeralds, a bag of coins—and each one was turned down by the king: "I have all of that now. What I want is a fountain."

Scene III: More small-group work, the struggle for gifts with more substance, a sense of the power of symbols in changing attitudes. Once more, there were presentations to the king, but this time, a villager cradling a baby in her arms.

DB: *What are you offering me?*
STUDENT: My student, your highness.
DB: *I have children of my own.*
STUDENT: This baby has a star on her forehead and can predict the future.
DB: *Stand over here, then, beside me.*

What deepened their work now was the opportunity to rework or relive the experience, the realization that the king had everything already, and the time that allowed for gestation of ideas. In the final group presentation, a strong young girl marched boldly up the aisle, and shouted:

STUDENT 1: O King, do not build the fountain.
DB: *And why not?*
STUDENT 1: Because he says not to!
And from the back of the room came a boy with his eyes closed as if he were blind, his arms outstretched.
DB: *What do you want, Blind Man?*
STUDENT 2: I have a message for the king.
He presented me with a small scroll, held by a hair band.
DB: *You can neither read nor write.*
STUDENT 2: It came to me in a dream.
I opened the paper and read.
STUDENT 1: O King, be a good king.

Reflection

Of course, the fountain would not be built, and the cheers of the students evidenced the duality of role: their pride in working as a Grade 1 class to conquer a complex problem and their success as villagers in thwarting the insensitive dictates of an unfair ruler. Drama lives in that dichotomy of role—the self and the other—as they blend. That class cheered for childhood's future victory and drama's power, and *The King's Fountain* was rewritten, retold, relived, remembered.

Demonstration: Letters to the King—Finding the Point of Departure

Having explored *The King's Fountain* with a group of Detroit teachers new to working in role, I was not surprised when one Grade 4 teacher chose that text as her unit for the required project in her own school. But I cannot forget the results of her classroom work, when she brought in the findings of her exploration to share with her colleagues. Her class had chosen to write to the king as village tribal elders, and she assisted them as the one who supplied the materials. And what letters!

The teacher told us that the point of departure in the story for her students was the old man's fear that his language was not equal to the king's, and their subsequent work was based on the attempts of the villagers to use elevated, formal language structures. The letters demonstrated her strengths as an art teacher as well, as the students used calligraphy on parchment, illuminating their initial letters, and struggling to find the words and the syntax appropriate for addressing a king. The text of a few of those letters appears below.

Dear King,

Your town, which soon faces destruction, is asking you if you would stop the building of the fountain. If you won't stop, we have some reasons why you should. Most of the people are too old to walk twenty miles to get water that their families need. The children are too young to get the water because they don't know their way to the east and the wild animals might kill them. The merchants want more for getting the water and want the poor to pay for that water.

Sincerely,
The Villagers

Dear King,

My people in the village below you hear you are making a fountain in front of your castle and we also hear it will take up all of our water for our pets, produce, and us. So, if you make a fountain in front of your castle, we won't be able to come every day because it is so far and we will die. So, if we die, you will have no one to rule or be kind to. So, please don't make your fountain. You won't regret it.

Sincerely,
Villagers

Dear King,

I write to complain about the water. I think it is nice that you want to make a fountain. But we do get water now. What about later if all the young members of the town go to work? Then we can't get it and it's always late at night. And they won't get it, they are tired. They will just get enough for themselves. I think you should make a stream going through the town.

Tim

I am amazed at these letters and aware of this teacher's great strengths in the classroom. She began with a story she had heard, helped the children develop a form of expression, and supported their attempts to find aesthetic and linguistic means to influence those in power. This last letter, however, remains my favorite—poorly written, but with brutal, honest strength.

> *Dear King,*
>
> *Your fountain is dum. It does nothing but kill people and when you go get the water our village will die.*
>
> *P.S. Knock it down.*
>
> *That's all king.*
>
> *David*

I asked the teacher about this last student. She replied that his comprehension of the activity was high, but that he did not hear the music of the words. She felt he needed many more stories and opportunities to represent and communicate his ideas. (And I had been afraid she might be concerned only with his handwriting.) Good teachers new to drama quickly understand this way of teaching and learning, and seem to have little trouble in adapting its strengths for their own classrooms.

Reflection

I want drama to deepen the students' understanding of themselves, others, and where they live, as they build an improvised world through a process of group interaction. Although I encourage them to create imaginary gardens, their response to the problems, conflicts, and characters must be real. How the teacher elicits both commitment and authenticity is what is important to true learning.

Demonstration: Drought—Building Drama from a Question

In a large school auditorium in Chicago, a group of third and fourth grade boys and girls sat with me as we discussed the rain outside and the land's need for moisture if drought was to be avoided. The students offered comments about the ecological balance that had to be maintained for a necessary food supply in a country where water was scarce. Taking my idea from the book we had not yet shared, *The King's Fountain,* I asked them why a leader might want to encourage a drought. The students in role became American reporters in a country in the Middle East, attempting to search for the reasons behind the leader's actions.

Here is what one teacher wrote of the demonstration session:

- It was great being in role with another teacher, because we could play off each other without giving the students direct information.

- This was a group ready to explode! They were truly thinkers. The close, quiet discussion of rain, water, and drought was intense and varied. The strongly worded question "Why would a man or woman want to make a drought?" plunged them to the heart of the drama and resulted in a wide range of responses from accidental pollution, to something having to do with "40 days and 40 nights." They were not afraid to challenge David, as when he came up with a reason and they all shouted, "Ahh, that's not true!"

- I liked the fact that we (the adults) were told the day prior to meeting these students that we were not to give them any direct information: that we were supposed to speak in riddles. After a discussion which started with the fact that it was raining outside and how some people pray for rain because of drought, the students were told, "Today in our drama there's going to be a very bad drought." They were also assigned their roles by David: "You are from another country . . . " ("American!" was called out by a patriotic young boy.) ". . . and you are reporters who have been chosen by the UN to find out what is happening in the east and why there is a terrible drought."

Scene I: In pairs, the students interviewed small groups of teachers in role as villagers, who had been asked to appear reluctant to reveal any information to outsiders. The students then reported back to me any knowledge about the situation they had discovered. To deepen their roles, I had requested that the reporters offer the villagers a drink from their canteens and try to win their confidence. For my part in the drama, I chose to remain as side-coach, out of role, but inside the drama.

Scene II: After the subsequent interviews, I removed the students from the auditorium while the teachers created a living fountain as a group theatre exercise. The student reporters then returned to view the mysterious factor causing the drought.

Scene III: In the next scene, the villagers shared with the reporters a prepared riddle about an eagle, which, through discussion, the students interpreted as a helicopter that the leader used to survey and control his people. After the students and I left the room once more, the teachers built, through collaborative movement, a helicopter with rotating blades and sound effects; when the reporters witnessed its landing in the desert, they confirmed their suspicions of a military leader who was telling untruths to his people.

Reflection

As the bell rang, the drama drew to a close, with the students as reporters choosing to leave their fictitious country because of imminent war. This lesson was free-form in design and troublesome by its nature for many teacher-participants; however, never as teacher have I been more secure with a lesson, knowing that I could call upon my hundreds of experiences with the story over two decades.

Questioning to Deepen Involvement

Asking open-ended questions in drama will stimulate the students' minds. I ask questions that matter to me, as a member of the drama group, and as a teacher supporting the students. Rather than asking questions that require a "yes" or "no" or too obvious answers, the drama teacher supports the hesitant student, challenges the unthinking or joking response, and guides the drama into new areas of learning. Through questioning, the teacher can give purpose, direction, and shape to the learning activities. Questions help students become involved in and committed to the drama, and they help the teacher feed information to the students in an economical way.

In a typical story drama, I ask dozens of questions, not as "teacher," though, but as the one who needs to know. This switch in the role of a questioner is very useful in drama for now I am able to ask a student a question to which I don't know the answer, to which there is no single, correct response. Instead, I am part of the drama, asking for the students' viewpoint and their interpretation of the ideas evolved so far. I want to be a teacher in drama who encourages and promotes the students' ideas, who acts as a catalyst in order to stimulate their minds or challenge their joking responses. I want to use my questions to help them think of new ways of entering different areas of the drama. I want the questions to be real, to be authentic. As in a real conversation, we ask questions that need to be asked for clarification. If I list my questions on a paper before I begin, they never quite fit into the transitional work.

If we think of the functions of questions, then perhaps we, as teachers, can find those questions that will help the students dig deeper into their work.

Types of questions

Questions that seek information:

• What must you take with you?

• What are we going to do about it?

• How many horses do we need?

• What kind of food shall we take with us?

• How should we plan the robbery?

• Where do you think we should place the stove?

Questions that assess student interest:

• Where might we all be together in this village?

• What problem is uppermost in our minds?

• What part of the story is the most interesting?

Questions that require students to seek information from books, documents, or other adults:

• Where does Toronto get its water supply?

• How did a Roman housewife dress?

• Where does a Navaho woman do her baking?

Questions that help the students to supply information:

- How many gallons of water should we take on the journey?
- Do you have a kiln to fire your pot?
- Are we well supplied with blood plasma?

Questions that call for group discussion to decide among several courses of action:

- Shall we be in the past, present, or future?
- Should we stay by the wreck and build a fire, or go out and look for help?
- Do you two want to decide this, or should we call all the householders together for a vote?

Questions that control the class:

- How can we keep the king from hearing us as we sneak past?
- How are we going to make ourselves look like soldiers?
- Are we too tired to start on the hunt today? Had we better just rest?
- Can you all hear what this person has suggested?

Questions that establish mood and feeling:

- What sounds can you hear in this old building?
- What do you remember about the times you had in this village as a child?
- Where will you put your belongings in this dark, unknown cave?

Questions that help the students build belief in the situation:

- Do you have the equipment necessary in the mine?
- Which computers do you robots have in order to control the planet?

Questions that deepen insights:

- What people will we miss now that the bridge to the mainland is gone?
- What would you have me do, as king, to make up for my misdeeds?

Questions that encourage reflection:

- What sort of leader will we need?
- On this journey, where did we need stronger leadership?
- What other ways could we have dealt with the forces against us?

Often the best question is simply a statement or a suggestion, because it motivates the students into responding. And of course, if you work in role, you have another thousand voices that can ask the question.

As might be expected, the most significant questions are asked by the students.

Chapter 6: Creating New Stories Together Using Drama

The very nature of drama ensures that students think in fairly sophisticated ways. The first element that trains thinking skills and a controlled use of emotion is, no doubt, the taking on of another person's perspective, or a "role." The perspective that the students take is then used in the service of other types of thinking. In order to participate in the drama, the students do more than learn specific facts: they process information and translate it into the drama form, and they draw on their imagery and experience, and seek to communicate that to others. The perspective-taking experience requires students to translate their learning into responses understandable to others. Drama can provide an evocative context for the expansion of feelings and ideas.

Building an Imagined World

Students create alternative selves, alternative lives, and alternative worlds—in play, in storytelling, and in drama. They rethink, modify, and supplement their everyday experiences through their experiences in role. As students deal with the problems and decisions that arise in the drama, through their interactions as an ensemble, they may bring their understanding of the outside world into the classroom.

This created work of art grows through trial and error as the participants explore the issue or event that has grown out of sharing a story. Somehow, the ghosts of the original story lead the students in a parallel yet different set of circumstances; the conversations and behaviors of the students in role give rise to a story framework that everyone feels as if they own. And when the process is complete, the drama story sits beside the original, and the students recognize the patterns and the people in both, and yet see themselves in the one they have co-constructed. We are stronger story makers for having moved into our own virtual story world, which we set alongside the original.

Demonstration: Decision of the Tribe—Considering the Implications

Willi Baum, the author/illustrator of *The Expedition*, has used a series of pictures in a cartoon fashion to tell his story about a tribe on an island and what happens when other people arrive. The pictures focus on a band of

Many of the stories and songs are as old as the hills, and possess some of the same earth-browned warmth and wonder that nature cherishes: others were minted today and stink of gasoline fumes and pulsate with the rhythm of engines. But all of these bits of language have a commodity they share: they are the voice of men telling us about themselves—the dreams, the wars, the yearning for love, the tricks and sly pranks, the banquets and crusts, the prayers for peace, the rape of mountain and river and the thousand-faced creation that each of us is.

Ramon Ross in *Storyteller*

marauding soldiers who invade an island, plunder a temple, retreat to their boat with their spoils—a stone temple—only to discover that their own steam engine has been stolen by the island's inhabitants and placed where the islanders' temple used to be.

Behind the pictures, there are rich stories to be explored. The reader enters a new world and constructs a society that is only hinted at, never seen in actuality. The story drama lies in developing these unknown people—their life, their work, their tribal celebrations, their lives and the conflict that results when strangers representing another culture arrive in their land. Because the people on the island are not pictured, we can develop their lives and their civilization as the basis for roles in story drama. "How will their lives be different from our own?" "What will their beliefs be?" "What will they believe about the seasons, the sun, or the new visitors?"

Many teachers are unsure if they will be able to draw their students into drama, but taking time to speculate, to work on ideas, to imagine together, can bring strong results. In order to develop the role of the tribe, we can decide on some of the important rituals in their lives. One picture shows a temple that has been dismantled. "What could it have been used for?" "Would it have to do with sickness or the seasons, celebrating war, or honoring family events such as birth or death?"

Scene I: Working in groups of five and six, Grade 6 students created one of the rituals that would have gone on in the temple long ago. I played a recording of Paul Horne to create a suitable atmosphere. The groups worked simultaneously, and I assisted when necessary. The rituals were all religious in nature, based on archetypes from the students' own experiences. I led the groups into a circle to represent the temple, and narrated the students through their demonstrations of the rituals, questioning them about their ceremonies. For example, one group had raised someone from death by plague: "Would a plague victim have lived if the new world had brought medicine to the island?"

Scene II: Next, the students sat in a circle and one by one, volunteers narrated the story of the islanders' first encounter with visitors, as it was told yearly by the tribe in order to represent the dangers of outsiders finding their island.

Scene III: In role as a tourist leader, I addressed the class as the tribe whose temple had been desecrated. I promised to bring them the inventions of civilization if they agreed to my plans to develop the island as a tourist centre. In groups, the students discussed the reasons they would give for refusing or accepting my offer. Next, in whole-class discussions in role, the students struggled with the dilemma, the girls wanting the new technology, and the boys refusing to be subjugated by an outside force. The class was extremely agitated about having to make a decision, and left the room debating the problem: "Will he ruin the bird sanctuary?" "Will the beaches be destroyed with oil spills?"

Scene IV: I returned the following week and the students' energy was still focused. They had to vote on accepting or rejecting the tourism proposal. I gave each member two marbles—a white one for yes, a red for no—and

To me, creating a story drama is like painting a large mural; we know the topic, but how the individual pieces will fit into the whole theme is the excitement.

76

each student went to the centre of the circle and placed the marble of choice in a dish. The tribe rejected the modern world.

Reflection

I received this letter two weeks later from the student who had acted as spokesperson.

> *Dear Mr. Booth,*
>
> *When we were talking about The Expedition, you asked us if we would let you come to our island, and bring civilization. You explained that meant building us hospitals, giving us technology, but in the same time you will have to cut down some of our trees, build casinos and bring in unknown diseases.*
>
> *I had no objection to this proposition, but I did not like the idea of you destroying the environment on our island. At the very end of our discussion you said, "Fine, I will leave you alone, but sooner or later other nations will find out about your island and come to you with war instead of peace." This started me thinking. In conclusion to the discussion, there is only one result: we will give you our knowledge, some of our gold and natural resources. In return you will give us your knowledge, electricity and protection from other countries that want to wage war on us.*
>
> *Yours truly,*
> *Andrei*

He had changed his mind. Why? What had happened when I left? Did the drama continue? What pressures were brought to bear? Did Andrei actually reflect by himself on what had happened and rethink his own view of the problem? Slowing down the work enables the children to consider its implications thus far. Through a rehearsal, such as the building of the temple histories, or through foreshadowing future events, we can allow a class to channel its energy without damaging the potential for genuine drama to take place.

Demonstration: Still the Leader—Revisiting the Story

A Grade 4 class in a tough urban setting created their own story drama from *The Expedition*. The young girl who role-played the tribe's leader demonstrated great solemnity and composure during our work.

In these four letters, you will see the outgrowth of the class's reflections, helped by a fine teacher's writing program. Note the two entries by the student as leader, the second one in response to her listening to the class debate in role the issue of whether to accept the restoration of the temple by foreigners. She has strengthened belief in her own role and in the dramatic conflict, and her writing is powerful evidence of her learning.

> *Dear Captain,*
>
> *It is me the leader of all my people. I have made my decision. It was very easy for me to make. My decision is going to be I will not take the temple from you because you*

seemed very strange and you were mean and why would you offer me my temple unless you are very sorry about what your grandfather did? I am not sorry about what I did to your grandfather. Thanks to your grandfather if he didn't take the temple I wouldn't take the top off your ship.

Your enemy,
The Leader

Dear Captain,

I agree with our leader not to take back our temple because I don't trust you and your king. Plus, what if it's a trap? We'll suffer even more. So don't bring back the temple.

(P.S. Throw that old looking temple into the deepest sea you can find.)

Your enemy,
The Cubby Man

Dear Captain,

I've made a decision. I disagree with the leader. I think that you should bring it back. The people are dying. There has been some mysterious drownings. People are catching the flu and diseases and we can't figure out why the babies are born so small. This is the reason why I want the temple back.

Yours truly,
Cinqaina

Dear Captain,

It is me again. As you can see, some people did not agree with me. One even wanted to overthrow me but the rest of my people didn't want the temple. So that means I am still the leader. Don't return to the island. My decision is made and my people agree with me and will stand by me. If you return, you will be hanged.

Still the Leader,
Power Woman

Would I had her strength and confidence in both her social position in the class and leadership inside the drama.

Reflection

When the students own the work, my role in the classroom becomes different. My energies can be devoted to strengthening those students on the edge, side-coaching them to enter the circle.

Demonstration: On an Expedition—Redirecting the Drama

The Expedition launched a story drama lesson with 11-year-olds in Australia. My friend and colleague, Phillip Taylor, videotaped and transcribed the lesson. Excerpts from his transcriptions appear here.

My job as drama instructor is to help the class find a way of entering the world they are about to construct. I begin very tentatively, searching for the moment when we can begin working in role.

Scene I

Philip Taylor from NYU has analysed this lesson at great depth in his book *The Drama Classroom: Action, Reflection, Transformation.*

DB: *Who are the people who had the temple originally?*
STUDENT: The natives.
DB: *Let's call them indigenous people. These indigenous people lived on the land quite a long time ago from the look of things. And do you know anything about these people? Do you know anything about their behavior, about what they did? Robert?*
STUDENT: I don't know.
DB: *That's right. We didn't see them once in the whole book.*
STUDENT: They're pretty smart because we didn't see them.
DB: *What else did they do that demonstrates their cleverness?*
STUDENT: They knew that the temple would be nicked as they nicked the ship's steam engine.
DB: *Were they fair?*
STUDENT: Yes, somebody took theirs, so it's . . .
DB: *So, if someone steals something of yours you can steal something of theirs?*
STUDENT: Yeah, equal.
DB: *I wonder what the police would think of that? If somebody steals your bike, you can steal their bike?*
STUDENT: Not exactly like that. This is different, because there's no laws for that.
DB: *There are no laws for temple stealing?*
STUDENT: Yeah, there is.
STUDENT: Nah, not really. These people, they didn't care.
STUDENT: They took their plans for the temple. They had probably worked hard on them a lot.
DB. *So, it would depend on whose law, would it?*
STUDENT: Yes.
DB: *In our drama today, would you rather be the invisible people or the people who stole the temple? You can vote. Who would rather be the people we don't see?*
Ten students have raised their hands while the other four have voted to be the 'invaders.'

Scene II

DB: *So, for today we'll begin by being those people. We know little about them, but we know one thing: You had a temple, you used it, valued it, and when it was gone, you rebuilt it with whatever you could find. As these people now, you will move ahead in time by a hundred years, and those who stole the temple will come back to visit you. I will role-play the stranger. You're going to have to choose someone to speak to me as leader. I don't know how you choose your leaders. I don't know if they're to be men or women. I'm going to turn my back and let you decide whom you want to be leader, whom you want to speak to me.*
Deb declares that she has accepted this leadership responsibility.
DB: *The leader does not have to speak; the leader may be so powerful that she has lesser people to speak for her. So, you have choices, Deb. You can speak if you wish. Maybe the leader is never seen.*

DEB: Will my people kick up a big fuss about the stolen temple?

DB: *Well, you might, or you might not care anymore.*

STUDENT: Do our people speak English?

Booth suggests that although a hundred years ago no English was spoken on the island, he will be able to speak their language, even though it is another dialect.

Scene III

DB: (In role) *People, thank you for coming to greet me. I shall make my other men wait in the launch. I appreciate your kindness in bowing to me, but I want you to stand and be on equal terms with me. I come as one who asks forgiveness. Who is your leader? I have come to return your temple.*

DEB: And that's supposed to make everything better now.

DB: *No, it's to remove guilt from my country. We are trying to make amends. On the ship, out of your view, I have the temple in pieces, with architects and design- ers who will reconstruct it flawlessly and give you back what you lost.*

DEB: Why did you take our pride and joy in the first place?

DB: *I apologize for having come from a nation who saw that as their duty in the past. I was not born then, and we have learnt so much since then.*

Some boys in the rear whisper and point at Booth.

DEB: Why do you return it after all these years? It's like you kept it for just as long as your people could look at it. Is there any damage to our temple?

DB: *The temple was taken apart stone by stone and taken to my country. We have brought these stones back to be rebuilt. You must understand that in my country we rebuilt your temple, we used it.*

DEB: In the same style?

DB: *We do not know how you used it here. We had to use it in our own way. But we have cleaned it up, taken it apart, brought it back and we're going to rebuild it on your island for you. It is our gift.*

DEB: May I please have a conference with my people?

Her people gather around and whisper inaudibly.

DB: *Excuse me, leader, you will notice that I have come unarmed and my launch is unarmed. However, the ship around the harbour is heavily armed.*

While we talk, some of the people whisper, "Skin him." Deb says, "Ssssh" in reply.

DB: *I'm sorry, but I must return and it's getting dark. I shall come back here in the morning.*

DEB. We want to see our temple, to see if it's all right.

DB: *I shall return it in the morning with that information for you. I appreciate your kindness and I shall leave you with this tiny gift for when I return.* (Booth offers an imaginary gift in his cupped hands.) *Take this gift, leader. Open your hand.* (Deb refuses.) *You don't want the gift?*

DEB: Can I please know what it is before you give it to me?

DB: *Yes, it is a medal from my ruler for the leader of your people. Do you want the medal?* (The people confer.) *You wish it?* (Booth hands it to her.) *You may hold the medal as a symbol of my ruler's honor. I'll be back in 24 hours with the temple.* (Booth turns away and then steps out of role.)

Scene IV

During their reflection time, the students out of role confirmed their suspicion of the visitor. The temple, they believed, was a fake, lacking in spiritual significance for them now.

The task for the students was to seek logical decisions based on immediate confrontation. Indigenous cultures throughout time have endured the indignity of usurpation and dislocation. The islanders of the story have been threatened twice by an invading army, once when their temple was pillaged, and now by the invaders' successors who are determined that the temple be returned. In an ideal world, the islanders might ignore these hostile overtures, but the drama confirms the real presence of the marauders.

Robert, another student, suggests that his people call their god for advice. One boy, Sam, assumes the role of the god and confirms that the temple is a fraud. He urges the islanders to avoid brutality but send a delegation of three representatives to the visitor's ship. Deb now rethinks the delegates' mission, fears treachery, and insists that she speaks with her people. Deb is constantly checking out strategy with her fellow islanders.

When the visitor returns alone, the students exploit this opportunity by capturing him, claiming that they need to find out more information from him. I stopped the drama in order to handle the imminent confusion of my being taken prisoner. I needed to regroup the drama, so that we could safely proceed.

Scene V

> DB: *I was just realizing how absolutely brave you are as a tribe to take me captive again, because, of course, you have all of them [the foreigners on the ship] waiting at sundown, don't you? Do you think they won't move on you if you have me? Is that it?*
>
> DEB: Well, you have to be important because you . . .
>
> DB: (Challenging) *Oh, really? I have to be important? What if I'm their pawn? What if I have been sent to you by them? What if I'm not important at all? What if you've just been condemned to death? What if I've told you everything? What if I don't know anymore? How are you going to make me "spill my guts" as you say? You're the one who imprisoned me.*
>
> STUDENT: Well, you could go back and get more information for us.
>
> DB: *You want me to spy for you? Why should I spy for you?*
>
> STUDENT: (Contemplative) This whole story is pouring into different compartments.

We work out of role for the moment.

> DB: *What do we make of these different compartments? How do we make sense of it?*
>
> ROBERT: I don't know. I'm just telling everyone before it goes too far.
>
> DB: *What if your tribe doesn't have any more ideas? You've captured this person. What is it that you're going to do with him?*

Scene VI

When a student proposes that I am to be hypnotized by the islanders, the students begin to make a case that their people have spiritual strength.

I notice my own goosebumps appearing at the oddest moments in teaching, when a youngster in the class speaks briefly yet stops the action in the room for a milli-second, when the class becomes silent out of respect for their own work, when the young actors coalesce with the directed energy of an ensemble. Tiny moments that only teachers recognize, teachers who must remember to cover their arms, lest the rest of the world notice the goosebumps. This is one of those moments.

The discussion concludes when I agree with the students that the strongest witch doctor in the community will hypnotize me in an attempt to uncover why the islanders should not take the temple. In role, I have been subjugated, conquered by the islanders who now probe my mind for the damaging information it might contain.

The students have selected the most timid girl in the class, Susan, to embody the one who transfixes, the all-powerful one who can mitigate time and mind. They will suggest questions for Susan to ask me while I am in the hypnotic trance. Ironically, Susan's face is hidden by her hair fringe, a reminder of her isolated and withdrawn place in this group, a fact later confirmed by her classroom teacher who seemed mesmerized by Susan's uncharacteristic posturing.

SUSAN: Sit down. What do you know about the temple?

DB: (Hypnotized) *The temple is real and a fraud. Within the stones are the voices of your people and they say to give you the temple, but also within the stones are the voices of my people.*

The group members begin whispering among themselves and help Susan find the question that will most reveal the visitor's mission. She listens as the questions are whispered to her and selects those which she believes will reveal the truth.

SUSAN: Why are you giving it back after all these years?

DB: *We need to put something on your island to control this area.*

SUSAN: Why do you want the island?

DB: *We need to control the ocean.*

SUSAN: But why do you need to control the ocean?

DB: *We need a base here.*

SUSAN: But why this island?

DB: *Because this island lies between the two great lands.*

SUSAN: Which two great lands?

DB: *The two great lands to the east and to the west.*

SUSAN: What happens if we do accept it?

DB: *You will have your temple back and we will have your island for a base.*

SUSAN: What kind of a base?

DB: *I am not to tell you this.*

SUSAN: Is it a base for war?

DB: *Yes.*

SUSAN: Against who?

DB: *Against any enemy.*

SUSAN: Why do you need enemies when you can have friends?

Scene VII

The students terminate the hypnosis, refuse the temple for a third time, and choose to live with the fear that their offer of friendship will be of no use in the face of an aggressor.

DB: (Out of role) *When I began this lesson, I did not know what I know now, that the weapons of mass destruction contained within the temples stones were created through their work. You drew from me this strange story. You were in charge of what happened in your drama. I was a participant, and I was challenged in my own thinking, just as you were. To me, creating a story drama is like painting a large mural; we know the topic, but how the individual pieces will fit in to the whole theme is the excitement.*

Reflection

The context of drama allows students in role to initiate meaningful talk and wield authority, and they may gain understanding from their own frames of reference, free from the language expectations and control of the teacher. Learning opportunities are altered by changes in the relationship between the teacher and students. As students interact inside role, they can explore social functions of language that may not arise in the language forms of the traditional classroom. The context plays a part in determining what they say, and what they say plays a part in determining the context.

This drama lesson is the only one in which I have been hypnotized. It represents a clear example of teacher in role: you act as a member of the drama ensemble and also work as a teacher, noticing the students in their story roles and in their life roles, so that you can instruct through the drama, planning and organizing the work, and ensuring the safety network of the class. I can (and did) stop the drama action wherever I felt the need, explaining or redirecting the students so that the work could continue. The class was deeply connected to the work, and I felt in control as the hypnotized teacher-artist.

Structuring a Story Drama Event

In story drama, we translate the experience of the story that was used as a resource and shared as a class into opportunities for developing a drama unit, a series of lessons, each building on the previous ones, evolving into a strong drama creation:

- Discuss the story with the students, helping them focus their responses towards the areas of interest that will form the basis of their play-making.

- Select several incidents from the story to enact or dramatize.

- Help the students choose situations that will connect them to the theme of the story.

- Determine the techniques, forms, and conventions that will help structure the development of the work.

- Mine the riches of the resource for details, information, and tensions that can add to the depth of the drama.

- Use the ideas, the questions, and the role playing of the students to enrich the work and to determine the direction the drama can take.

- Add tension whenever possible by establishing mood and atmosphere to support the role playing.

- Reflect on improvised scenes both in and out of role in order to build stronger frames for continuing the work.

- Incorporate written forms, visual arts, and mask making to construct dramatic scenes.

- Draw the different scenes to a conclusion that represents the work that students have developed.

- Create opportunities for reflecting upon and connecting their improvised drama to the curriculum and to their lives through discussion, journal writing, and art.

Helpful prompts for structuring a story drama event

See also *Drama Worlds: A Framework for Process Drama* by Cecily O'Neill.

During the lessons I create with the students, I hear myself using many of these statements and questions to help organize the action of the drama. These statements and questions act as prompts for finding ways of rethinking and redirecting the work in progress. I may ask one student in role to clarify his or her position, or I may ask a group to replay what they have created so that we as a class can interpret their suggestions:

- *(Repeating their words)* Is that what you said?

- Is that what you meant?

- What are the implications of what you have said?

- What are the implications of what you have done?

- What do others think about their actions?

- Show me the effect of what she has said or done.

- Remind me of how this work began.

- Reminisce about your lives (in role) before this event began.

- What happened in the past that affected this action?

- Flash back to the incident . . .

- Flash forward to a future . . .

- Freeze the action so that we can see what is happening.

- Ask someone about an action or a statement you saw or witnessed.

- Talk aloud and all at once about your responses to what has happened.

- In groups, revisit and replay the scene where . . .

- Gather as a group to observe the scene where . . .

- With a partner, explore what happens when . . .

- Create a frozen picture of . . .

- Alone, create the scene where . . .

- In a circle, one by one, comment on the story so far.

- In groups, draw a diagram of . . .

- I will be working in role alongside you as . . .

- This is a story of a group of people who . . .

Chapter 7: Writing Inside and Outside the Drama Experience

Two questions can help us frame the connection between drama and writing:

1. What does writing do for the role player?
2. What does drama do for the writer?

Imaginative involvement in drama can be a powerful stimulus for writing, and that writing, in turn, can serve several different purposes in the drama work. The best drama—and the most effective opportunities for linking writing with it—emerge over extended periods, during which students have time and incentive to work their way into a unit, to refocus and change direction; and to edit and present their creations to trusted and understanding others. Through the process of writing in drama, participants can give form to their feelings and ideas and learn not only to express their views, but also to re-examine and reassess themselves in light of the reading audience who is working in role. Young people begin to think of themselves as writers who control the medium in order to say what they want to the people they want to reach in the context of the drama.

I have found that when writing is embedded in a context of personal significance for the writer, the writing skills will be enhanced. If students are engaged in the expressive and reflective aspects of drama, living through "here and now" experiences that draw upon their own life meanings, then the writing that accompanies the drama and the writing that grows out of it may possess the same characteristics and qualities.

Writing within a Concrete Framework

The concrete framework provided by dramatic situations can both encourage and enable students to compose and transcribe for authentic reasons. The discussions and reflections arising from the possibilities and explorations within imagined and felt situations can lead to a variety of written activities. As well, many drama conventions lead naturally to literary conventions:

• A town meeting can result in a transcript.

• A witness can create a monologue.

• An incident can become a piece of reporting.

Writing generated in response to the concrete particulars of the dramatic context can be connected to real human situations. We write to plan what we might do, we write to support the dramatic action, we write to consider what we think we have accomplished within the drama, and we write to reflect on our shared experiences. In these ways, writing and drama are linked inside authentic classroom learning events.

Drama serves as a catalyst to help students tap resources they may not have known they have. As students enter into problems and conflicts, they imagine themselves as other people, thinking their thoughts and feeling their responses. They begin to view situations from outside themselves and see the consequences of actions from a new perspective. Once the setting is in their mind's eye and reflected in the lives of the characters they have created, they can transfer these processes to their writing.

Within drama, the students can explore all the writing modes, including free writing, journals, interviews, brainstorming ideas, lists, letter writing, announcements, proclamations, and petitions. They can report about events within the drama, design advertisements and brochures, devise questionnaires and important documents, and write narrative stories that are part of or conjured up by the work that was created. As well, many opportunities are provided for collective writing, where members of a group work together on a mutual enterprise, such as collecting data or organizing information, all in a meaningful context.

Demonstration: What Coyotes Have to Say—Writing from Remembered Role

In Shelley Peterson's *Untangling Some Knots*, which is published by the International Reading Association, there are some excellent articles on developing strategies for teaching writing. In "The Tangle of Context: Meaning Making in Role," I describe in greater detail this coyote lesson concerning writing in role.

I have worked with the picture book *Coyote Winter* in dozens of primary classrooms and with hundreds of students. The prologue for the story explains that the text and illustrations are a memorial to the author's sister, Doreen White Elliott, who taught in a Hutterite colony in Alberta for many years. The German-speaking Hutterites, with a history of being persecuted for their religious beliefs, live on large, collectively owned farms. They work their farms together and eat together. As the author writes in the prologue, "The Hutterites are a peace-loving, industrious, Christian people. Doreen loved them, especially their students. The events in this story may not have actually occurred, but the story is certainly true in spirit."

Animal life is usually of interest to students, and authors and illustrators present events and issues in their books that work well for drama explorations.

Coyote Winter by Jacqueline White
Fox by Margaret Wild and Ron Brooks
Coyote Autumn by Bill Wallace
Wild Dogs by Deborah Hodge
The Trap by Marc Talbert

In almost every case, the students' responses in drama have concerned the fate of coyotes in the cruel leg-hold traps still used by the Hutterite farmers; however, these schools where I worked were located in inner-city Toronto, far from the habitats of the wild creatures. The challenge posed by the story is evident: how could we explore the construct of the story, in which a teacher and class release a coyote pup from a trap, so that the students would understand the complexity of the trappers' situation? Often I would role-play a farmer interviewed by the class in role as reporters, who had heard about the incident; the background information about the damage to farm life created by the coyotes would lead to problem-solving situations as the students attempted to alter the dynamic of the confrontation between the ways of the Hutterites and the need for the animals to survive.

Our role-playing sessions have included

- the teacher being interviewed by the Hutterite school council about her actions

- the farmer being questioned by reporters about the inhumane leg-hold traps

- the teacher being let go from her position by the principal

- the family of the boy who told reporters about the experience being brought to task by the school board

- the farmers inventing new methods of handling the problems of the coyotes

- the Hutterite husband of the teacher discussing the incident with his wife

- a documentary revealing the customs of the Hutterites

On several occasions, while working with groups of student teachers and a demonstration primary class, the students, after listening to the story, interviewed families of Hutterites—the student teachers in role; then, at intervals, I would gather the class together for sharing the information about the trapping situations. The many participants led to a variety of responses by the students, and the conversations were lively and passionate. As I listed their ideas and insights on chart paper, the issues engendered by the story and the visuals grew and deepened. After the lesson, the students wrote to me and, depending upon the teacher's instructions, the writing revealed an unusual awareness of the complexity of this conflict between a culture and a creature.

Writing that illuminates the drama

Drama allows students to use reflective language in the classroom for a greater variety of purposes than many areas of the curriculum allow. Its very nature encourages students to imagine, predict, hypothesize, and evaluate as they explore situations, solve problems, make decisions, create new contexts, interpret new information, and reassess previous attitudes.

On every occasion, the classroom teachers I worked with recognized the need for reflective writing and enabled the students to record their feelings about the work in poem, story, letter, or visual arts.

I read what the students write and come to see both the story and the drama through different lenses. After they are freed from the imperatives of my lessons, students reconsider their own experiences through reflective distancing and remembered role. I find they often resort to talking to themselves through the medium of the poem or the letter, thinking with a pen or a mouse, while altering forever my personal meaning making from our time together. In my opinion, both parties benefit. I read what they wrote, first as a reader and second as a teacher, and my drama work alters as I change.

Prompted by both the story and the drama experience, the students reflect in writing. They clarify and interpret their thoughts and feelings as they replay and rework the events and the possibilities that have been opened up through the dramatic exploration. The drama work helps them crystallize their felt knowledge, and continues to influence them as they write from what might be called "a remembered role," after the events, but with the experience still affecting their work.

The students now have a hybrid role: that of spectator-participant. With the shadows of their dramatic roles still having influence over them as writers, students can produce powerful and evocative writing. The students are sharing their moving commentaries on the story and the drama, having left mere recounting and reporting; they are using written conventions to represent their shift in attitudes and perceptions, extending personal viewpoints inside a broader and more complex frame. Their coyote voices are heard above the classroom, echoing down the hallways of the school, connecting us to the world outside the education institution—the ultimate destination of every student.

I am coyote. My leg is sore.
It was nice that she let me free.
So I could live and make more babies.
I hope I never fall for it again.
I hope my cubs never get caught.
I am starving to death.
I hope that I will survive.
My blood is pouring out.
They will not win.
And I will do my best to fight with my fellow friends
I need to find somewhere to live.
I need someone to help make my foot better.
I have to find my pack of coyotes. I want to go home.
I want to get back at those farmers.
It's hard to find my mate.
I hope my babies are healthy.
I am in a lot of pain.
I am ready for dinner.
It's morning.
We will fight tonight.

Dana (age 9)

I am coyote. I was freed today.
I was playing around. I howled at the sun.
I was freed by a nice lady and some kids
I do not know why they told me go,
nor understand what I was trapped in.
Now I am alone, bloody and wet.
I need to find my mother: I looked up.
I thought of the mean man who made that thing.
I went to the barn. I found a coyote.
She sniffed me then picked me up in her teeth,
carried me to a hole, trapped me in.
I was with my mother.
She licked my wounds for two days. I recovered.

Linda (age 9)

I am coyote.
I don't think the traps are good
because you trapped my cub in one of those traps.
Why do you try to kill us?
We are just living things looking for food.
We are wild animals
We have to hunt for food to keep alive.
My child is dead.

Melissa (age 9)

I am coyote. I have lost my way.
Suddenly I saw a chicken in the snow.
Of course, I was hungry
I walked toward the chicken when
I felt this sudden pain in my leg.
I looked down and saw some metal jaws digging into
   my skin.
I though my life had ended.
I lay down and waited for the hunters to come.
I felt sad and helpless.
I thought about the warm den in the forest
and I thought about my mother,
who would wake up and start looking for me.
I had been laying for nearly an hour
when I heard some voices
Now I thought my time had come.
But when I looked up I saw a woman with lots of
   children.
I was scared.
To my surprise the woman was trying to free me.
When she did I licked her and tried to do something
to make her understand that I was trying to thank her.
But the children chased me away.
At first I did not understand.
Finally, I understood Danger was near.
So I left but I was sad.
I had lost my mother
and didn't have anybody to take care of me.
I roamed the forest for the rest of my life keeping away
   from man.

Simon (age 8)

The thought, discussion, and writing that occur after the drama may be as important to learning as what happened during it.

Reflection offers a chance to be heard, an opportunity to express ideas and feelings, and an occasion for language. While drama is an active, "doing" medium, the reflective mode allows students to make meaning: they examine and understand their thoughts and perceptions both as spectators and participants. "Analogous reflection," as the prominent drama educator Gavin Bolton calls it, transpires when students relate the information and feelings learned from a drama experience to another situation. This generalization may occur much later or be revealed informally in a seemingly unrelated context.

Teachers as reflective writers

As the teachers work in role within the drama activity, perhaps as a member of the community, as reporters or as farmers, they can also participate in the variety of writing events that are integral to the drama. In one lesson, the teacher's contribution to the letter to the village council deepened and strengthened the impact of the drama. In the following example, the teacher submitted her own reflective monologue, writing alongside the children from her remembered role.

> *I am coyote and I hurt*
> *My paw is numb my leg sore and tingly.*
> *I lick my wounds but will they heal?*
> *I am hungry but do I dare to go in search of food?*
> *I should go back to the den*
> *Perhaps mother will heal me.*
> *I must be careful.*
> *I thought the world would be an interesting place.*
> *A place to explore and play.*
> *Now it is a frightening place;*
> *problems exist for me that I hadn't thought of before.*
> *I must be cautious, play less, move carefully.*
> *I wonder if my leg will heal*
> *before other animals find that I am hurt.*

Franca (teacher)

Reflection

As I review and reflect on my own work in drama and writing inside classrooms, the "remembered role" recurs as the strategy most frequently chosen by the students themselves. They try to make sense of what has happened, still inside the memory of their roles, drawing upon the spectator-participant relationship of those who were involved in real pretending, which is, of course, the heart of childhood play. The writing that grows from "remembered role" may reveal much more about the students and their experiences than traditional reflective discussions built around the questions of "what I liked" or "what I didn't like." Supporting the development of emotional intelligence includes creating and sustaining opportunities for reflective consideration, so that the coyote voices are heard once in a while amid the present contexts of students' worlds, reminding them of who they were at one moment in time, and encouraging them to build upon all of their past experiences.

Demonstration: Vodnik and Manya—Speculating on an Old Tale

I look for new tellings of the fairy tales to begin our drama explorations, alongside authentic collections.

Vodnik by S. Zavrel
Snow White by Trina Schart Hyman
Snow White in New York by Fiona French
Into the Forest by Anthony Browne
Complete Brothers Grimm Fairy Tales
Complete Hans Christian Andersen Fairy Tales

"Vodnik" is an Eastern European folktale about a creature of the lake who wanted to marry a mortal, Manya. Its central conflict is the heart of a story drama unit. What tales have people told about Vodnik? How did the stories begin? Why were the stories not forgotten? These three questions became the focus of a dramatic activity in a Grade 1 setting.

Scene I: Through group discussion and storytelling in role, each family in the class "village" made up the mythic origins of the creature. The stories were supposed to be told by the village members late in the evening, as volunteers from each group shared what they had created. In an attempt to draw tourists to the village, an imaginary museum was built, displaying these stories, and a photographer took publicity photos of the creations (tableaux created in groups and photographed by a student). Signs were written to warn people of the dangers and to create interest in tourists. Each family allotted part of its home for tourist facilities and made advertisements for these facilities.

The village planned a giant surprise party for Manya on her twenty-first birthday, since she had no family. A student volunteered to role-play Manya, and each family brought a gift, a treasure from its own heritage, as well as a special dish to the dinner. The villagers sat down at banquet tables in the town hall, and the gifts were presented to Manya. Minimal props were used—most of the action was mimed. People passed around the food, and drinks were served.

Then there was a knock at the door. When a student in role as mayor answered, in role as Vodnik I entered the hall and demanded to marry Manya. I stated that I would return in one half-hour for the decision. When I had left, the mayor announced that the village would have to decide if Manya should be helped. There was much discussion in role, as the villagers feared for the safety of their children and for their own lives.

Scene II: After the discussion, I presented Manya with the situation: if she volunteered to marry Vodnik, the village would be spared. After some hesitation, Manya offered to go with Vodnik. The village refused to allow this, though, and plans were hatched to save her from this fate. One family offered to hide her; another felt that if she appeared to have a terminal disease, Vodnik would leave; another decided to make a "Manya balloon," filled with grenades which, upon being touched, would explode, killing Vodnik. Others attempted to build traps of various types. At length a plan was voted on and adopted: a large net would be placed on the ceiling of the town hall. Manya would stand in the middle of the room as bait. As Vodnik approached her, a signal would be given, Manya would dash to safety, and the entire village would reach up, grab the net and pull it over the creature, thus trapping him. The plan was engaged.

Scene III: In role as Vodnik, I knocked at the door, a volunteer answered, and I took her hand. This caused the crowd concern, since they realized two people were about to be trapped in the net: the volunteer as well as Manya. The boy who was to give the signal looked around in panic, unsure of when the net should be pulled. Suddenly the signal was given, and Manya ran from Vodnik. The volunteer who had answered the door pulled free and escaped. Vodnik was trapped, amid cheers from the villagers.

Reflection

After the completion of this drama work, I read the entire book to the class. In their follow-up writing, carried out in the classroom under the direction of the teacher, the students were asked to speculate on Vodnik's origins. In the cases below, one can see the specific impact of the drama on four different students.

> *Vodnik was a mean person. He kept people in jars. In the picture you will see Vodnik's weapons and him. The needle is for shrinking people so they can fit in to the jar and there is no way to get out of the jars.*

Maxeen

> *Once there was an ugly, slimy animal and his name was Vodnik. He is from the ocean and he was born in a shell and he goes up every night in to the village and one night he opened a door and there was Manya. He said, "I will marry you," and he went to the ocean where he lives and he said to Manya, "I will be back in five minutes," and Manya was scared and she did not know how she could get out of it. She went to the village and she said to a villager, "Can you keep me in your house?" And she did do that . . . The end.*

> *Thank you,*
Jana

> *Long ago there was a frog up in space. The space frog kicked the frog out of space and the frog fell into the lake. The frog sealed people's souls into glass jars. No one knows where they are.*

Philip

> *Dear Mr. Booth,*

> *I liked the play very, very much. Did you like the play too? What part did you like best? I do not know what part I liked the best. Thank you for inviting me to do the play with you. It was one of the best plays in the world. Thanks very much! Thanks for inviting the class too. I think the class liked the play very much and I think that they liked you very much too. Did you like the class too? I liked you. Did you like me too? We did a better story than the book did. Do you like the story that we did better or the story that the book told? Well?*

Caleb

The writers in these examples used the reflective composing time in unique ways, as they sought to describe what had happened, investigated motivation for the actions of the characters or pondered the reasons for the results of the whole interactive process. The drama provided context for the writing; the writing illuminated the drama work.

Educating the imagination is a difficult and complex task, and it is a slow developmental process as students work in the written mode. Drama can help give them skills in using processes that may transfer to writing.

Chapter 8: Finding Strategies for Supporting Literacy through Drama

No one in real life "reads reading"—everyone reads for a purpose. Every word is a process, and the reader is as important a part of that process as the text. As in drama, the reading experience is personal: readers understand what the words say to them, translate the experience they read about into their own contexts, and respond with feelings and attitudes about the experience and the text. It is common for teachers to discuss the knowledge relevant to a text—awareness of the source, the author, traditions, and techniques. However, not much time has been devoted to those qualities that the reader brings to the text—feelings, experiences, attitudes, values, and beliefs.

The student's awareness of possible meanings and patterns is vital to that student's reception and production of language, and the student derives this awareness from hearing and using language. Educator James Moffett said that raw experiences and human socializing are the bases from which verbalization and literacy are derived. One does not need to be able to read and write in order to comprehend and compose language. Obviously, both can be done orally, by preliterate or illiterate people. Meaning is a larger, lifelong matter, connected to literacy only because letters symbolize speech. Meanings are learned through one's total life experience and no more by reading instruction than in any other way. To derive full comprehension, a reader must become the co-author, absorbing the concepts presented and then scrutinizing and assessing those ideas in the light of personal knowledge and experience.

The true relationship between drama and reading is much deeper than just making the former an adjunct to the latter. Although the term *drama* usually appears in manuals used in reading series and in reading texts, the activity suggested is often an introduction to the reading selection, a follow-up activity, or an outgrowth of the reading lesson. At best, drama is seen as peripheral to the reading program. What is meant by drama in such materials is not clear. Often the "drama" activity is simply a word game or a physical exercise to release tension. How drama influences the student's reading comprehension has seldom been examined.

Negotiating Meaning

The relationship between the areas of drama and reading lies in the world of meaning. It is the idea of symbolization and its role in the discovery and communication of meaning that connects drama and reading. Both

Many devices used in school to train readers to note exact details in a text may result in producing readers who, in making the effort to come more closely to grips with the exact meaning of an author, abandon the attempt to relate the significance of what they read to their own social lives.

Jeffrey D. Wilhelm's *Improving Comprehension with Think-aloud Strategies* is a related recommended resource.

areas are concerned with interaction. In story drama, the students enter into a dialogue, modifying and exploring symbols by changing and challenging each other's contributions. When reading, they enter at first into a dialogue with the author, then with other readers, and finally with themselves. Through discussion and analysis, they modify and develop their understanding of the author's meaning, as well as absorbing the diversity of meanings their classmates have taken from the text. In both cases, students are negotiating at the symbolic level.

The drama work must elaborate on facts to find hidden truths and universal concepts, not just retell events from memory. Weak drama, like weak reading, is concerned with words rather than with the meanings behind them. Going beyond the text requires that the teacher's techniques somehow relate the concepts in the text to the student's experiences. In this way, fundamental memories brought forth by the intensity of the reading or drama experience are tapped: the resultant response is both personal and universal, and can be shared in the context of the literacy situation and the dramatic experience.

Demonstration: Danced to Death—Entering the Print

I was working with a story in the students' reader, "The Dancing Tigers," by Russell Hoban, which uses the folktale idiom to deal with the problem of modern society's encroachment on nature. In the story, a Rajah disturbs jungle life by bringing taped music along on a tiger safari, and in revenge, the tigers "dance the Rajah to death." I read the book aloud to a Grade 4 class and shared the illustrations with them. In our subsequent discussion, the students expressed interest in the confusing time frame.

Scene I: How the Rajah dies is suggested in the book, but when I asked the students how he had died, they were unable to tell me. They had been unable to make sense of this crucial element of the story. This gap in their understanding seemed a suitable place for beginning the drama inquiry.

Scene II: Since drama is a tool for unlocking meaning, I chose a role as the Rajah's son who had returned from America to discover the reason for his father's death. The students in role as trackers and servants gave me various explanations about his death, conjectured from their own knowledge, but unrelated to the story. Eventually, two students volunteered the information that the Rajah had been danced to death. In role, I angrily rejected their responses, claiming that I no longer accepted such superstitious beliefs since I had been educated in North America.

It was now up to the students to prove the truth of the story to me—I had ordered them locked up until they disclosed the real reasons for the Rajah's death. Out of role, I worked with the students in groups as they planned to explain to the Rajah's son what had happened on that safari.

Scene III: When we returned to role, the students demanded the opportunity to prove that the Rajah had indeed been killed by the dancing tigers. They asked the son to accompany them on a similar safari, where similar music would be played, and when this had been agreed to and the ensuing drama had begun, everyone was sitting with me in a circle. Then two

We must provide opportunities for the reader to realize that other child readers of the same text have found different ideas and understandings in it.

The blending of fact and fantasy is a valuable resource for helping students create parallel worlds through drama. Russell Hoban's *The Dancing Tigers* is one example; *Riding the Tiger* by Eve Bunting is another.

students, as tigers, began the Dance of the Silence That Is Partner to the Violence. As we watched, I was suddenly taken by both arms and told politely to leave the tigers or I would meet my father's fate.

Reflection

The students had understood the concept of the tale. By teaching me, they had unravelled the threads of information and come to grips with an experience outside their own frame of reference. They had made sense of the story by reliving it through drama. Thus, an elaboration of the story led to a more thorough examination of one of the story events. As the students took on the roles of the servants, they brought to the drama not only all they knew about the story situation, but also all they knew about being questioned by authority, and all they knew about innocence and truth.

For more than a dozen years, young people who, on first reading, could make no meaning of the Rajah's death, have, with the drama, fought for their lives with this previously unbelievable piece of information.

Demonstration: The Mission—Making Text Connections

This lesson is explored in greater detail in an article of mine, "Reading the Stories We Construct Together," in *Literacy Alive! Drama Projects for Literacy Learning*, edited by Judith Ackroyd.

In a demonstration involving a class of primary students from an urban Canadian school, I chose to read a story aloud and provide copies of the text for use during the drama exploration. My goal was to have the students "consider a story," that is, to examine its impact, make connections with their personal worlds, respond to the thoughts of others, and reflect upon the implications of the author's words.

We began with a discussion of robots, drawn from students' media experiences, and we listed these on chart paper. Then I read to them the short science-fiction story "Men Are Different," by Alan Bloch.

Men Are Different

I'm an archaeologist, and Men are my business. Just the same, I wonder if we'll ever find out about Men—I mean really find out what made Men different from us Robots—by digging around on the dead planets. You see, I lived with a Man once, and I know it isn't as simple as they told us back in school.

We have a few records, of course, and Robots like me are filling in some of the gaps, but I think now that we aren't really getting anywhere. We know, or at least think the historians say we know, that Men came from a planet called Earth. We know, too, that they rode out bravely from star to star; and wherever they stopped, they left colonies—Men, Robots, and sometimes both—against their return. But they never came back.

Those were the shining days of the world. But are we so old now? Men had a bright flame—the old word is 'divine,' I think—that flung them far across the night skies, and we have lost the strands of the web they wove. Our scientists tell us that Men are very much like us—and the skeleton of a Man is, to be sure, almost the same as the skeleton of a Robot, except that it's made out of some calcium compound instead of titanium. Just the same, there are other differences.

It was on my last field trip, to one of the inner planets, that I met the Man. He must have been the last Man in this system, and he'd forgotten how to talk—he'd been alone so long. Once he learned our language we got along fine together, and I planned to bring him back with me. Something happened to him, though.

One day, for no reason at all, he complained of heat. I checked his temperature and decided that his thermostat circuits were shot. I had a kit of field spares with me, and he was obviously out of order, so I went to work. I turned him off without any trouble. I pushed the needle into his neck to operate the cut-off switch, and he stopped moving, just like a robot. But when I opened him up he wasn't the same inside. And when I put him back together I couldn't get him running again. Then he sort of weathered away, and by the time I was ready to come home, about a year later, there was nothing left of him but bones. Yes, Men are indeed different.

Scene I: Working in small groups, the children were asked to create "an instant replay" of the story, without the benefit of a general discussion where they could share their responses. Observing their "silent" re-enactments, I noticed that all 10 groups seemed to understand the climax of the plot, where the character of the robot had unfortunately operated on the human, causing his death. In the follow-up class talk time, the children generally commented on the issue of the robot's attempts to help, without realizing the consequences of its actions. They wanted to know who the Man was, why he had travelled to that planet, how the robots had come to control the planet, and if other humans had ever visited the planet. By now, the children were deeply inside the text, considering the imagined events, making sense of the print.

Scene II: We, as a group, selected the issue of the Man's origin as the basis for the continued drama exploration. The class had not yet left the text—they were digging into it, mining it, continuing to ask "what if." In small groups, the children brainstormed how the Man might have reached this planet, what his reasons for visiting the planet could have been, and what had caused his "malfunction." As the children worked, I interacted with each group, working in role, asking them to respond to me in role, as they developed their scenarios. Frequently, the children revisited the copies of the text, looking for meaningful cues.

Scene III: The children gathered in a large circle to observe the interpretations of each group and consider how they added to our collective understanding of the original story. As Co-ordinator of Interplanetary Explorations, I took part in the dramatizations. I questioned and supported each group's role playing as they presented their projects to me in order to receive funds for travelling to the planet of robots. Usually, one or two children acted as spokespersons and through questioning in role, I was able to involve other group members in the work. They watched each presentation, observing the differences, adding to their story context, and building a greater print world.

Scene IV: The following day, the teacher asked each group of children to retell their proposal plans by writing letters to another teacher, recounting their drama experiences. The following examples demonstrate the language and literacy strength of these young students:

We're sending 11 people, including you, on a mission to find life on another planet. You will be going for ten days we will give you enough oxygen for 18 days. If you find life, try to observe it and if it hurts you, use the lasers we will give you.

Alison and Michelle

Were sending 1 person. The mission is to get to the disk that they are using on the planet. It holds lots of secret things. Like if they are going to attack and destroy our planet. It is very important because we need to know. We don't want them to destroy our planet because it is our home. We want to stay alive for a long time, so we can change some things.

Evan and Adrienne

We are sending 3 people to an uninhabited planet. A doctor, a botnest and an astronaut. Their mission is to identify and retrieve a certain plant that can be dried and ground up to make an ointment. The ointment will be used to cure a plague. If they do not succeed, they will go to planet 5.0.6.5, to get a substitute. They will take with them: 30 days worth of oxygen, 40 days worth of fuel, and enough food for 25 days. Their mission will take 20 days.

Didi and Tommy

Your mission is to go to another planet. One man has been there before and has never returned. With video tapes we have received we know the man had landed on the planet. We do not know if this planet holds life. Just in case something deadly lives on this planet we will arm you with dangerous high voltage lazers. If the mission succeeds and you bring back the missing person, you will be paid 10,000 dollars.

Drazen and Billy

1. We have to kill the aliens.

2. We sent two people on a mission kill the aliens.

3. We want the aliens' D.N.A.

4. You will have oxygen for 20 days and you will go for 10 days.

Mitchell and Justin

Reflection

The research on intertextuality tells us that we make meaning by connecting the many texts that we have experienced—print texts, life texts, media texts, story texts—and constructing newly interwoven stories. In their writings, these children reveal bits and pieces of the books they have read, the television programs they have seen, the stories they have heard, and the selection we were exploring. I was surprised by their choices of words, the scientific terminology, the awareness of trade and commerce, and their burgeoning knowledge base of nationalism and imperialism.

The story text we begin with, whether read silently or told aloud, becomes part of the child's meaning making, and as ideas are tried out through interactive responses, the reader/listener deepens, extends, reconsiders, modifies, and reconstructs a personal world view. All of this can happen with a significant literacy experience, supported by teachers who employ drama to expand the interconnections occurring when children meet a story.

From my own work with students over the years, I have come to recognize the power that drama can offer to a story experience. After working with several text selections, in similar activities, students are more likely to explore a story on their own, wondering about the writer's ideas and methods, and wandering among the dozens of text experiences that the story triggers. Literacy teaching, so I believe, involves encouraging students to make meaning with printed text through emotionally connected interactions. Drama strategies offer us exactly such opportunities.

Demonstration: The Tiger's Snare—"Working" a Role

Tiger was written by Judy Allen. Her book, *Seal,* also works well for story drama.

The picture book *Tiger* offers opportunities for distancing the cultural frame of drama participants. Participants can look outside their life contexts and yet move into drama in an easier fashion by placing themselves in the imagined world. I used this story with a group of teachers in New York, teachers who knew much about language arts and who wanted to move drama into their programs. I read the story aloud to them, shared the book's amazing pictures, and then we briefly discussed the events of the story.

Scene I: The teacher-participants role-played a group of teachers from Des Moines, Iowa, enmeshed in a village conflict and anxious to leave, having seen the military handling of women. But their tour bus could not yet depart because the driver was too frightened by the military outside the village. The teachers found themselves in the furor over stories of men who would hunt tigers for flesh and fur, risking the future of their families.

Scene II: I changed the roles to those of the women of the village. The participants could now use the elements of the story they had heard. The women of the village gathered in family groups to discuss the story of the tiger that had been circulated by the children to the village schoolteacher. Their talk focused on the danger of such rumors filling their boys' minds with false notions of manhood and of the need to hunt tigers for meat and fur. Some wives felt under their husbands' dictates, others valued the old ways, and still others manipulated their men into following their wishes. But all felt drawn into the tiger's snare.

Scene III: The conflict between the men's need for the tiger hunt and the government's decision to forbid it found voice in the complaints of the women about their men's attitude towards the hunt. Some families claimed that the powers gained from eating the tiger were only in tales, but others had seen the burial mound of those thought to be killed by such marauders of the jungle. Dissent seemed to weave its way among the huts as the women worried themselves into a wailing chorus of fear.

Scene IV: Suddenly, the women were called to the village centre by military officials, lined up, and questioned about their connections to hunting tigers—an endangered species—an act considered illegal by the international trading community. In role as the leader of the military, I interviewed several women who answered with silence. After expressing anger at my authority being challenged, I issued a warning that those found guilty of hunting tigers would be removed from the village and imprisoned.

Scene V: Now, half the participants role-played mothers; the other half, children. The mothers called their children into their huts and attempted to put a stop to the tales of tiger hunting shared with the schoolteacher. They considered banning storytelling by the children outside the family safety circle. They asked the youngsters to compose stories about the different ways in which fathers could demonstrate courage other than by killing tigers, and the children created a tale of respect and admiration for sensitivity and compassion in a man.

Scene VI: The women approached me as the teacher in his schoolroom and questioned me about the stories of the children and their being noticed by the government. I defended my position, explaining how vital telling life stories was to the education of the children, and described the book I was arranging to be published in support of my literacy program. One mother suggested that the children could suffer because of this book and the school could disappear. I told them that I would reconsider my position and look into the matter.

Scene VII: I narrated this conclusion to the drama:

"When the men returned from the rice paddies, they found the hunter in the village taking pictures and they put him under house arrest, charging him with lying to them about his hunting of the tiger, and blaming him for the visit by the military.

"The tiger, meanwhile, remained free, except for the photos found in the hunter's pictures of the creature in a variety of poses, sunning himself, scratching, attacking a bird and hunting in the camouflage of the jungle. In the last photo, slightly out of focus, the tiger appeared to be dancing with joy."

Reflection

These teachers had come such a long way in their responses in role to the reading of *Tiger*. I had kept them in a role close to their own experiences, but they quickly moved into working as the villagers, and through their improvisational dialogue, determined the direction and the focus of the drama scenes. The story from the book gave them information and context for building a powerful drama event, and they understood the power of working a role to bring meaning to print.

Demonstration: Story Chants—Reading Aloud in Drama

A few years ago, the Michigan International Reading Association invited me to take part in its annual conference. Rather than addressing the delegates, though, I was to work with the students of Detroit. The committee felt that a conference devoted to reading should begin with an event dedicated to the students who might benefit from such an affair. It was decided that there should be a participatory reading experience followed by a circus performance: I was to conduct the former, and Ringling Brothers/Barnum and Bailey Circus would provide the latter.

I hesitated to accept the offer. The sheer number of children—more than 3,000—was daunting. The challenge proved too intriguing, though, and I found myself in an open-air arena on the banks of the Detroit River with thousands of children in front of me and a microphone in my hand.

I had decided to tell an African story that involved four different chants and had distributed copies of the chants beforehand, each on a different-colored sheet of paper. At the appropriate time, I would call out, "Pink Papers" or "Green Papers," and those children with the right papers would provide the required response. I had not counted on the volume of the chanting, and the response was overwhelming. With thousands of children chanting and clapping on cue, the story took on the attributes of a ritual.

As I was nearing the end, I looked up, and around the amphitheatre stood the circus people and animals—clowns, acrobats, elephants—all drawn by the chorus, watching the performance of the children, a setting by Fellini. For me, it was a powerful event, where reading aloud was completely embedded in story, and where story was alive and well, being lived at the moment by 3,000 children.

Beyond Reading Aloud to Interpretation

I look for books that provide opportunities for students to read aloud in dramatic contexts and then for the class to move into dramatic events. *Alice Yazzie's Year* by Ramona Maher is one such book.

I have found that reading aloud can be connected to drama in four ways: (1) sharing rehearsed selections that may lead to dramatic exploration; (2) reading aloud selections that have previously been the basis for dramatic exploration; (3) reading aloud in role pieces within the drama (letters, proclamations, points of debate, songs and chants); and (4) reflecting orally about the drama from personal journals, poems, and related materials that may illuminate the work. Most students need assistance in working in an oral reading situation, and drama strategies have provided me with great support in this area.

Few scripts for children are available in schools, but novels, poems, and picture books can be excellent sources of good dialogue that may easily be adapted for oral reading activities. Children can work in pairs or in small groups, reading the dialogue silently and then aloud. Teachers can alter the experience in several ways. For example, they can have the children change roles, they can introduce new settings or tensions, and they can change the time period. The goal is to help students dramatize the selection in such a way that they can discover new meanings in it.

Readers Theatre is a technique for reading aloud stories and poems as if they were scripts. The actual words are used, and the narration, along with the dialogue, offers a set of exciting problems for students to explore. The simplest method is for some students to act as narrators while others read the bits of dialogue. When students begin to omit such lines as "he said" or "replied John," they are beginning to work with the interpretation of the words, touching upon the sense of theatre that such an activity develops.

There are dozens of options, however. For example, a character who speaks dialogue may also read the information or thoughts found in the narrative that refer to his or her role. Several characters can read narration as a chorus or repeat lines as an echo or refrain. I am always amazed by the ingenuity of students when faced with making "out-loud" sense of a narrative selection. They see it as a puzzle, to be tried and treated until the whole picture is evident. With some physical arrangement, such as stools for the speakers or a pool of light within which the group can work, Readers Theatre provides a perfect opportunity for oral interpretation, as well as a vehicle for dramatic exploration.

The selection used for Readers Theatre can then be used within the drama work as a stimulus or source of tension that adds to the playmaking. The exercise of creating a Readers Theatre demonstration can serve as the beginning of the drama work, as the students build on events to create a frame for dramatic exploration.

Drama can be a means of releasing young students from "the tyranny of the script," allowing them to examine the themes within the printed text they have been given. Improvisation based on a text becomes a tool for the exploration of the original text's ideas, relationships, and language. It is important that much of the drama be not just the oral reading of a text, but a living through of its concepts.

While in role, students can read aloud poems, songs, excerpts from novels and stories, or their own compositions, and can explore various interpretations of them. Working in small groups, students can select the interpretation they wish to give the words. They can even devise ways to express the text in dramatic terms, establishing spatial relationships among the characters, and making specific recommendations (about tone, volume, and pace) on how the words should be spoken.

Inside the drama structure, participants can read aloud documents, parables, lectures, and excerpts found through research where the role play gives added strength to the belief and commitment in the work. They can respond with the words of others to support their own ideas and viewpoints, feeding new strength and tension to the dramatic unit. In a unit on mining 100 years ago, for instance, court documents of related articles read aloud provided a powerful stimulus for continuing role play.

In short, story drama can present text as "earprint." Some print longs to be said aloud, and we can bring words to the ears of our students in dozens of ways.

Demonstration: From Print to Potions—Dramatizing a Poem

A Grade 5 class was exploring the theme of wizards as part of its language arts study. As a guest instructor, I had read excerpts from Ursula

What students write from within the drama can serve as the basis for Readers Theatre with another group, either as an integral part of the work or as a reflective activity after the drama. Transcripts of improvised work, either tape-recorded as the action takes place or re-created by scribes after the event, can help students to see the cause and effect of their role play, while providing materials for other groups to read aloud.

Le Guin's *A Wizard of Earthsea* and then chosen the following poem by Agnes Buckles as a basis for some drama work:

Sorcerer, sorcerer, what do you brew?
Sweet, sweet, honeyfield dew.

Sorcerer, sorcerer, who is it for?
Boys, girls, a dozen or more.

Sorcerer, sorcerer, give some to me!
Drink, drink, magic you'll see.

Sorcerer, sorcerer, what will it do?
Wish, wish, it will come true.

In a large multi-purpose room, the students gathered to hear me read the poem aloud, using a different voice as questioner and as sorcerer. Next, in pairs, all working at the same time, the students read the poem aloud, one reading the sorcerer's lines, the other reading the words of the visitor. They then changed roles.

I asked each of the students playing the sorcerer to create, in space, a cave where the sorcerer concocted his potions. The visitor would arrive at the cave seeking to have a wish granted. The students enacted the scene in pairs, all working at once. The sound of their voices filled the room, and each pair dramatized the poem, oblivious of the others.

I then asked the students to change partners and gave the next set of instructions: the sorcerer was to convince the visitor to drink the potion so that a wish could come true; the visitor was to decide whether or not to drink it. Although the visitor determined the wish, only the sorcerer would know if the wish would bring the visitor good fortune or danger—people must be careful what they wish for. The pairs read the poem aloud and then froze in their final positions. Some of the students playing the sorcerer had used powerful movement as persuasion; others had made the words enticing and evocative.

About half of the visitors had accepted the potion. Then the sorcerers announced the secret of the spell to the visitors, who responded with shock or laughter, according to the meaning of their decisions. The students gathered around the teacher and discussed the reasons for accepting or refusing the potion, and the sorcerers described their plans for encouraging the drinking of the magic elixir.

Whole class responding to the teacher in role: I then role-played the sorcerer, and the class responded in unison as the visitors. The students, as a group, decided on their reason for visiting the sorcerer, out of my earshot. Then, the sorcerer appeared to discourage the visitors from wanting the potion, and the class's determination to gain control of the wish grew. Finally, the students surrounded me as the sorcerer and began chanting, "Drink, drink," and I gave a sample to each student in turn. They then began to transform from visitors into sorcerers, the outcome of their private decision, thus taking control of the wish-granting powers.

The drama had begun.

Reflections

I have been reading aloud with students for more than 30 years now. I read, they read, we read together, we echo each other, we make dialogue into script, we chant, we sing, we demonstrate, we share moments, we delight in words, we repeat, we whisper, we shout, we read and move our bodies, we read and clap our hands, we read to those who can't or don't, we read what they don't have or can't see, we read to reveal information we have found, we read to make a point, we read together as a ritual of belonging, we read from our memories, without print, we read to hear the sounds of language, we read to give others our own print ideas, we read to change direction and refocus, we read to find the voices deep within the well, we read to raise our own voices in tribute to literacy and language.

Storying Aloud

We read aloud what we've written, excerpts from other stories that we loved or wondered about, words that touch us or puzzle us, tales from before, stories about today and tomorrow, episodes from people's lives, poems that cry out for sounds in the air, letters from friends, stories about places where we have never wandered, stories about dogs and horses and mothers and granddads and eccentrics and students and school and city and countryside, stories of hope and death and wonder and fantasy. We read short stories and long stories and chapters that build up the tension for days. We read stories from album covers and music sheets, blurbs about writers from the backs of book jackets, titles, reviews, and recommendations.

We read aloud, we fill the classroom with the voices of our ancestors, our friends, our novelists, our poets, our records, our documents, our native people, our researchers, our journalists, our ad writers.

Drama offers us dozens of opportunities for having our students read aloud in meaningful contexts. We may begin with a poem or a script, and then build the drama around the ideas in those words. Then, when students revisit the original selection, they bring to their oral interpretations new layers of meaning that deepen and enrich the words they say aloud. They story with their drama voices.

Chapter 9: Using Students' Knowledge and Expertise to Structure the Story Drama

Contemporary education is concerned with developing thinking processes in students. Every curriculum guide embodies this principle in its goals; every teaching workshop is related in some way to techniques for aiding cognitive development in students. What implications does this have for drama teaching, so much of which has concerned the "feeling" side of the learning spectrum? Is there room for encouraging thinking, for *demanding* thinking, in a drama lesson? Can drama fit within the academic curriculum? Can it be a basis for thoughtful learning?

Yes, of course. The arts tend to be associated only with the affective domain, but the cognitive should be—has to be—part of any teaching event. As we have seen, inventiveness and problem-solving can be developed through gathering information, planning and selecting materials, describing artistic problems, modifying and examining materials and information, experimenting with alternatives, and implementing solutions and sharing them with others. In this sense, drama is both a subject matter and a teaching approach of significant value in promoting thinking.

Balancing the Role and the Real

As teachers, we seek to help the learners move into unknown areas, developing hypotheses about issues and concerns that intrigue them, testing those hypotheses through problem-solving activity, and reflecting about the consequences of their actions. By being part of the learning, by interacting and dialoguing, students come to understand the process of imaginative inquiry. They act upon and take responsibility for their own personal changes and focus on human concerns, both as individuals and as members of society. Factual information, such as the death of the buffalo in the example that follows, becomes real to students through their involvement in the drama. They participate in decisions and in events that they have determined; at the same time, they consider the consequences of their actions and the impact of the information on their own lives and the world in general.

It is the balancing of the two experiences—the role and the real—that allows the students to make meaning, and it is this negotiated meaning that makes drama a learning opportunity. The students create new perceptions and understandings, modifying their existing concepts and attitudes from both outside and inside the experience and developing a subjective/objective relationship with the world. The students forge links with their real world and the world of illusion, making more meaning.

Using drama to promote language and thought

When drama is part of the Language Arts curriculum, it can foster

- interactive, co-operative language use during the planning stages (what is going to happen)

- imaginative, expressive language use during the drama in-role phase (what is happening)

- reflective, evaluative language use at the completion of the drama (what has happened, why did it happen, what could have happened)

By valuing the contributions of the students and by creating a language-filled classroom, the teacher can encourage students to use concrete language activities as a forum for developing thought. The students can move from their own subjective worlds to a more universal grasp of what they have been exploring within the drama; they develop the powers of both language and symbolic thought.

Since classroom drama generally works in an intimate atmosphere, often free from audience tensions, the participants are able to use a variety of language functions in a feeling/thinking mode: arguing, persuading, ordering, explaining, mediating, and organizing. As the drama work deepens and grows, the students can choose to move into more public and formal modes of speaking in role—addressing the townspeople, speaking to the king, arguing at a council meeting. Language, thought, feeling, and learning occur when the students have the power to shape the experience.

Problem solving is the basis of work in improvisational drama. The students respond to a situation filled with conflict through movement and speech. They are challenged to look at what is taking place in the drama for clues to how to proceed. Decisions about how a problem could be resolved may be made before or after the drama, but are best reached *during* the drama, when the students are most intensely involved in the situation.

The most meaningful solutions will emerge while the students are immersed in their roles as co-operators, planners, decision makers, and, ultimately, problem solvers.

Demonstration: Buffalo Burden—Making Tough Decisions

The drama lesson involved a group of Grades 4, 5, and 6 students from a summer school in the arts who had volunteered to work with our teachers on a drama course. In role as a tribe of North American native people, they had to make a decision about sharing their few remaining buffalos with a neighboring tribe. The source for this drama was *The Iron Horse* by Paul Goble.

After reading the story aloud, I asked the children to imagine a time when the Plains Indians had lost entire herds of buffalos to hunters. To these marksmen, the shooting of herds of buffalos from the windows of trains was mere sport. They seemed unaware of the buffalo's importance to native people.

Books by Paul Goble use the legends and the history of native peoples and lend authenticity to curriculum topics, which can form the basis for drama events:

The Iron Horse
Buffalo Women

The teachers on-course and the visiting children became "the buffalo." While I kept a beat on the tambourine, the buffalos grazed quietly, until the sound of approaching danger sent them stampeding. The group ran in place, creating a thundering sound. Then I used the tambourine as the sound of a rifle, and the older buffalos were shot one by one until none remained alive. While the adults remained motionless on the floor, I discussed with the children how the native people whose lives depended on an abundance of buffalos might have felt about this slaughter. The children were concerned that the settlers had killed the creatures so wastefully, while the native people had considered them sacred.

Now in role as native people, the children decided to round up the remaining buffalos and hide them so that the animals would not starve or freeze in the winter. I began to narrate: "Nobody knows this but us. And we know where the buffalo are, and we have them hidden. There might be another tribe that needs food, and that's who this group of adults will become. They're another tribe of native people on the prairies. Their buffalo have all been killed by the white hunters and they want animals to start their stock with. If we as a tribe give up our hundred buffalo, we will not have enough to replenish our own stock of animals."

We then divided into two tribes: the tribe without buffalos (the adults) and the tribe whose buffalos were kept hidden (the children). In the drama, the adults had to convince the children to share their buffalos. As teacher-narrator, I had introduced the context for the drama with a built-in problem: "Why would they want our buffalo? We need the hundred buffalo for self-sufficiency." In her journal a student commented later on the dilemma:

> I think that we should not trust the other tribe and not help them because when it was the buffalo hunting season the other tribe did not hunt for food but we did. Now they want us to give them our food. Yet if we have enough food we should help them out. The reason I think we can't help them is because we don't have enough buffalo for both our tribes. If that is the question— which tribe would survive—I think it would be the tribe that set out hunting for buffalo before winter season. It is also hard to see the other tribe die but if we could help them we would. Although if we hunt other things and join forces, we could hunt more and faster.

Working in role as a tribesman, I intervened to clarify the problem, questioning the children about possible solutions. The girls of the tribe with the buffalos wanted to take food to the hungry and medicine to the sick of the other tribe, but were persuaded by the boys not to sacrifice the buffalos, or their herd would dwindle. The girls shared with the others what little corn their own families had. The boys, however, didn't trust the other tribe and were angry that their food was being shared. I then added the information that only the women possessed the secret of where the buffalos were hidden. The leaders of the buffalo people were sent back and forth to negotiate with the other group, but in the end, they continued to insist that to survive their tribe alone needed the hidden buffalos.

As the class period ended, the children had still not resolved the issue to their satisfaction, and out of role, I summed up the drama: "This is a story about a tribe who had the wisdom to maintain their buffalo stock for their children's children. It is the story of a tribe whose women took food from their own children's mouths to help others in need. It is the story of a tribe who had a treasure, also a burden. Your treasure is your future, and you are burdened with it."

Reflection

Here is how one teacher summed up the experience:

In all of this it is important to note that David allowed the drama to evolve from student responses so that the story was theirs. (The students decided on the dance interpretation of the buffalo grazing, and the girl decided to share her food.) It was only on one occasion when he "shaped" the drama by maintaining that the hidden buffalo were still there and this input was essential for the drama to proceed.

His input as tribesman was interesting when he acted as challenger to the girls who had shared their food. ("You gave them half the food; now there is only enough for one family. You are endangering your tribe.") He also challenged one girl, accusing her of being a spy and suggested the others may have betrayed the secret.

This served several purposes. It immediately focused on responsibility and consequences of accepting a role. The implications of this role were immediately brought home to her and to those who rallied around her, thus serving to deepen their sense of belief, commitment and role play. It also intensified the drama by creating an additional inner conflict which forced students to move beyond an easy-ending solution to a complex problem.

During follow-up sessions with their teacher, Alistair Martin-Smith, the children continued to try to find a solution to their problem by setting out on a journey together with the other tribe, to find a place where they could hide the buffalo together so they would never be found by the settlers. During the journey, they learned to trust one another by sharing the difficulties which beset them. They painted maps of the journey so that they could one day find their way home, and they shared the stories they had written in their journals of how they received their Indian names.

The structure encouraged personal, verbal "immediate" reflection by a number of students. One girl made the parallel of buffalo killing with present-day duck-hunting. Another boy maintained that people killed for fun then because they had little to do in terms of entertainment (videos, etc.). A girl made a comparison with human frailty of the past and with the present condition for human error. Certainly, one of the questions each student must have asked was "What is our present-day connection with nature?" This was made clear when David pressed for information about cows and milking and it was obvious that few of them had any awareness of animals.

On a non-verbal reflective level, students were led to a consideration of loyalty (peers/group versus individual), to the motivations for killing (perhaps beyond hunting), and to a sense of what it feels like to struggle for survival in the face of technology (muskets). There could be an increased appreciation for the sense of the importance of life ("the tribe was wiped out—they are no more") and the nobility of indigenous peoples. It forces them to consider realistic choices one has to make in terms of survival. (Shall we live for the good and maintenance of "us" and does that involve negation of "them"?) Is there such a creature as a hero who could emerge from the drama and face our dilemma? Students can move from a consideration of the specific to universal themes and questions, thus deepening feeling/thought processes and broadening exploration.

Demonstration: History in the Making—Confronting Equity Issues

Redcoats and Patriots: Reflective Practice in Drama and Social Studies by Philip Taylor is a recommended resource for this type of work.

Nancy Steele's class at Horizon Alternative Public School in downtown Toronto engaged in a three-month drama unit called "Facing History," based on the equity and diversity components of a curriculum document, and focusing on the Holocaust and immigration of Jewish survivors to North America. The issues in this teaching theme are complex and difficult. I had the fortunate opportunity of watching the class at work for much of the time, planning with and observing the teacher in action, role-playing with the students on occasion, and documenting the inquiry processes used by the students. They were student researchers wearing the "mantle of the experts" in their role playing. Here is how Evelyn, one of the Grade 8 students in the class, wrote in role as a doctor:

In the article "Language Power through Working in Role," published in *Educational Drama and Language Arts*, edited by Betty Jane Wagner, I include other moments in this extended drama unit with the Grade 8 class.

Report

Canada First

Re: Immigration Duties on 11/03/46

   On November third, nineteen-hundred-and-forty-six, I, Dr. Evelyn Darling MD, was at the Immigration Office for Canada First. My duties as Chief Medical Officer were to check passports for valid landed immigration status, supervise Dr. Marvinel Laurie, my assistant, and perform medical tests on patients and decide whether they passed the health test, thus being in fit condition, not including any unknown/known diseases, and in perfect mental health.

Creating a context for drama

During the previous month, a library of novels concerned with the Holocaust had been set up in Nancy's classroom, and many students had read several of the books. The class also watched a documentary film, *America and the Holocaust*, about an American who, as a young man, emigrated from Germany and then tried to bring his parents to the United States to escape the Holocaust. The film provided background about this tragic event and helped establish the context for the work to follow. One of the students wrote this film review:

This movie was frightening because my understanding grew past what you read in books, past the imagination to the real thing. I know that this is someone who went there. The film was telling me this, that these are real pictures, that the person in front of me on the screen was there. We saw people standing as if they were dead, people beyond skinny. The narrator has seen his family thrown into one big grave and buried. To know that they have survived this horror means they must be the strongest people. When the movie was over the same feeling I had was printed on everyone's face around me. The silence was stunning.

Nancy, along with the integrated special education teacher, worked with two groups of students, setting up the framework from which the drama experiences would develop. At intervals, the two groups met together in a large group. The students chose their groups by drawing from a hat: they were to become either filmmakers or the families of the Holocaust survivors. The groups separated, and the planning for the ensuing drama began.

The filmmakers' group: Nancy set up the situation for the filmmakers, carefully including statements that would later add dramatic tension to the need for families to preserve the stories of their lost loved ones. She assumed the role of representative of the National Film Board and introduced the drama with these words:

The National Film Board is looking for young filmmakers to submit entries to its documentary film competition. The topic chosen for this year's contest is "overcoming one's past." We are asking for films that deal with Holocaust survivors who have decided to put their horrendous experiences behind them and "get on with their lives." There are many such people living now in Toronto who would probably agree to participate in such a film. We at the NFB feel that there have been enough films that dwell upon the horrors of the past and that films like this encourage depression and morbidity. We want, instead, to encourage young filmmakers to take a more positive approach, to show people who are willing to forget their past and move on.

The conflict that would form the basis for the later events began with this information, as the filmmakers were guided towards contemporary concerns. In small groups, they began to develop storyboards for the films they were planning, beginning with a video documentary of the urban setting of the school in a dense, multicultural market neighborhood, the actual home for many survivors from the Holocaust.

The family group: Meanwhile, in the second group, the family members were given the following instructions: Each family had saved two pictures from before the war; the first picture showed a relative as a child, with several other people, in a happy situation; the second picture showed the survivor at a family gathering just before the group was forced to move because of the war. Each of the families developed the stories of these pictures by using their bodies to create two still dramatic pictures or tableaux to depict their creations, drawn from their previous reading, discussion, and role playing. The family groups were brought back into a circle to share their family albums by presenting these tableaux. Students then wrote in role in their journals about what they had learned of their relative who had survived, about his or her childhood, creating the memories of the family before the war. The students were reminded that for the next class, they would need their completed documents for immigration, including a passport, a health certificate, and their full knapsack to represent luggage.

The first drama event: Immigration perspectives 1948

Nancy established the context for the first whole-class dramatic improvisation. The family members were to attempt to immigrate to Canada after World War II. (In fact, it was three years after the war before Canada opened its doors to a few Jewish immigrants.) The special education teacher was to be in role as a member of the Canada Jewish Congress who had come to facilitate the arrival of these people at immigration. She would be able to translate for the immigrants, who had each designed a passport and carried a letter from the Canadian Embassy.

The group of students who were filmmakers were now in role as immigration officers. Their job was to interview Jewish immigrants arriving from Europe. They worked in teams, filling in the Landed Immigrant Status forms for the immigrants before they could be stamped. They had to find out the immigrants' names, examine and verify their papers, and get them to sign a statement agreeing to a medical examination.

Communication was allowed only by signs (though they spoke about the immigrants to other officers in English). Immigration officers were warned to be especially wary of immigrants who might have false documents. Two students became part of the medical team calling out the medical exams (hearing and sight). Applicants with the TB stamp on their medical papers were not passed. Nancy in role acted as chief immigration officer.

When the drama was over, the students were asked to write in role. The immigrants described how they felt before, during, and after the interviews in diary entries they intended to save for their grandchildren. At the same time, the immigration officers wrote letters to the head of "Canada First," an actual historical organization, reporting on their first day at work. The role demanded that they accept being members of a group that, in history, had resented the immigrants. Here are some of the letters and journal entries:

Report to Canada First

Someone has got to take a stand and stop the amount of immigrants from coming into our country, 'CANADA.'

The immigrants will be prepared to take less money for jobs, and that will reduce our standard of living for everyone. New ethnic groups will move into our communities. Schools will have to teach new religions each day, and our cities will be separated into little communities of people who are of different beliefs and cultures. Our government will consist of different races, and since Canada is still a fairly new country we are still trying to figure out what it means to be Canadian and with new people running our country, it will be hard to know what makes Canada different and special.

My son and nephew both went to fight in W.W.II and both had to watch their friends being killed. Europe caused this war to happen in the first place and should take some responsibility for their own people. Foreign diseases will be brought into our country and we will have no way of curing them.

I hated the job I was given by Canada First as the intelligence officer, and stamping the passports that decided whether they would stay or be sent back. But we Canadians have to stand up for our country. Even if it does mean that we have to be cruel. I wish there was a nicer way of saying this, but immigrants will not help Canada form into the new great country that we hope it will be.

Kerry

Letter of Resignation

Dear Canada First,

I am deciding to resign from my duties as medical officer of immigration because I now realize that the health of my family and I are jeopardized. These immigrants are not like normal patients; they carry all sorts of diseases that span from the unsanitary conditions they lived in. These conditions include polio, TB, Infectious Hepatitis and malaria, all of which could be transmitted in an airborne manner. Having two young children I feel it is my responsibility to abandon work with these refugees and to take up private practice where these infections are not present. It has been a wretched week. We can't pass the immigrants because even if they are clear of infection, they could be carriers of lethal agents that lie dormant in their gastronomical tract or have disorders such as anemia or nerve system damage from cerebrospinal meningitis, that Canada's health program can't pay for. Not only does my job pose a danger to my life, but legally I should not pass anyone of this low quality health, rendering my job completely pointless.

Marvinel

Diary Entry by an Immigrant

I have passed the last step to my freedom. I am hopeful that the troubles I have experienced throughout the past years are over. I am free. Today I entered Canada. I am now reentered into the world of the free without fear of persecution. My new life begins now. However, this did not all come easily. The process of immigration was not enjoyable. I am afraid I have lost my dear friend Sara who was my only acquaintance in this new country. I am not sure when the separation occurred since the entire experience is a blur in my mind.

We were herded into a line and accompanied by our liaison, Mrs. Stein. For a very long time I waited in that line not knowing what was ahead. When I was finally into the room I was yelled at in a language I did not understand. Seeing the others ahead of me without shoes I removed my own in hopes that was what the officers were trying to communicate to me. Next I was at a desk with an officer yelling questions at me, again in another language. You will never know the feeling of not having any control over anything. Whether I was accepted or turned back was all in the hands of these men. At the next station I was subjected to a physical exam. Many of the people in front of me had not passed this exam and were forced into an area. I passed this exam and then was sent to another station where again I had no idea what was to happen. I passed this test and was sent to a waiting area. I was told by the others around me that this was the area for those who were accepted. And it was.

Now I have made it. As I said earlier, I was separated from Sara somewhere during the confusion. I have hopes that she, too, made it through, and, that I will be able to find her. For now I must concentrate on my new life. Maybe I will find a job, and I will try to learn their language.

Avi

Post-Drama Reflection

In the immigration drama, I tried to keep the routines and look professional. But deep down, I was most concerned by processing the immigrants. There was one small feeling even deeper inside that wanted me to be nice to the immigrants and pass them all, but my sense of duty greatly outweighed that feeling. I liked the sense of order we conveyed throughout the drama, but I actually felt anger towards the disobedient immigrants. When an immigrant was nice, I tried also to be nice without the teacher noticing. When an immigrant was mean, I felt that I had a right to actually punish them by detention.

Marvinel

The second drama event: Neighborhood under threat 1964

The work from the first event established the context for creating a community in 1964, threatened by change. The students worked in role as families of those immigrants who had come to Toronto, using the research gleaned from the preparation and the experiences of the first drama experience. Instructions had been given to all the students by Nancy:

> You must choose a job from the following list: board of education trustee; teacher at local school; local politician; leader of the Kensington Business Association; local religious leader (priest, minister or rabbi); leader of the Kensington Community Residents' Association; editor of, or reporter for, the local newspaper.
>
> You are concerned with the news of this neighborhood being demolished for the building of the munitions factory. Decide how you will best be able to stop this from happening.

Using the documentary video the students had previously filmed, groups in role began to develop as a classroom project a community of the sixties, its history and present status. Two weeks later, four student teachers and I visited the classroom to take part in a drama session as government officials announcing the planning of a munitions factory on the present site of the businesses and shops the students had spent much time researching, developing, and representing. The format of this session was formal and complicated, for the students were relegated to citizens with little power at a public meeting. For eighth graders, this resulted in much frustration and great learning. As we entered the room, a student handed us a newspaper broadsheet she had produced on her own in advance of the meeting.

> *The Kensington Times*
>
> *November 29, 1964*
>
> *News reached yesterday that the government is going to build a munitions plant in the Kensington core with a loss of about 30-50 businesses. The weapons made will be sold to the USA government to aid in the Vietnam war. The plant is scheduled to be built in 3 years time and the prints are already in progress. Re-location of citizens will be put into action in the near future.*
>
> *Public action is already being organized to defeat the idea of this plant. Mrs. Julia Ford, head of the Kensington Business Association, is "appalled that the government could do this to the thriving market . . ." The munitions plant will result in the closure of several area schools, pollution, and many health issues. However Mrs. Steele, leader of the Munitions Plant Project (MPP) denies that this project will do any long-term damage to the Kensington Community. Public outrage at possible Factory!!*

Because the class was constantly writing—summarizing, reporting, and editorializing—I will let Evelyn's words describe what occurred in the drama session:

> *A community meeting was held yesterday afternoon at Kensington Community School at Bathurst and College. Mrs. Steele introduced herself, Mr. Booth and his associates and the need for a meeting. Mrs. Steele said she hoped to bring the suggestions back to the mayor.*
>
> *We heard questions such as "Are you sure we want a munitions factory?" "The government had already confessed that they don't care about the community thus all they care about is money." "Who elected these people?"*
>
> *The meeting began at 9:15 as scheduled. I handed out the newspaper and took my spot next to Mrs. Ford and the meeting began. In the first part, Mr. Booth separated us into four groups, each meeting with one of his staff members.*
>
> *We were in a group with 'Lisa.' I suppose she went by first name basis hoping to gain our trust. Trust doesn't come easily. We addressed many issues*

forcefully, getting very passionate about most topics. She seemed strong but underneath I felt she was squirming like an earthworm.

Mr. Booth called the staff to a conference before we could talk further. The groups were a good way to express our feelings and to show 'Lisa' that we wouldn't stand down from our decision. We discussed many historical issues such as the Halifax explosion in the early 1900's, the Ottawa Munitions Plant which exploded, and other such worrisome issues. We also discussed (actually we told her) health and pollution issues as well as the big issue of resettlement.

We were soon called back into a big group meeting. Business leader J. J. Ford was the first speaker and expressed explicit concern over the relocation of businesses. The location of the plant was discussed but no locations were revealed. A local rabbi was deeply concerned about property values and the synagogue which may be destroyed. The Kensington Teachers' Federation spoke up and expressed great worry over schooling issues, but Mrs. Steele interrupted and stated the mayor was not concerned with the community. Mr. Booth directed the meeting making us look like uneducated fools who didn't know a thing. Unfortunately, no one stood up to him. If he had called on me again I would have told him the truth. I do not like Mr. Booth and I will die before I see my press and newspaper overrun by the likes of him.

The meeting was adjourned and we all stomped out of there with malevolent attitudes.

In role, as chairman, I was able to control the situation easily, calling upon volunteers to speak and silencing them when the action warranted it. I have seldom heard youngsters talk with such passion and eloquence. They fought to retain the neighborhood that they had researched and created in time and space throughout a few months, believing in the families they had created and in the lives they had lived through. For young people accustomed to controlling much of their program in the alternative school setting, the loss of power within the drama frame proved deeply frustrating and emotionally wrenching. They had been subjected to authoritative change both in role and in their own lives.

Speech Prepared for Town Meeting

I'm a rabbi and, as a representative of the Jewish community, I am extremely concerned about the proposed munitions factory. If we tear down all these buildings and build a munitions factory we will be faced with pollution, health problems, and my synagogue is in great danger. Once again we, the Jewish community, feel as if we're being pushed out of a place that we call home. Additionally, the value of our houses and properties will diminish and it will be difficult to sell our property if we are forced to move.

Nani

Journal Entry

The drama today, was for myself, the most powerful one so far. Everyone felt so strongly about what they had to say—myself included—I actually was so insulted when my family was called 'uneducated.' It felt so real, even though I'm not actually Jack Tannenbaum, and those people weren't my wife/daughter/sister—although, like the community of Kensington at the meeting, our school has provided the same kind of community, where, if something like this happened, we would stick together. I felt so stupid when he had my picture taken beside his assistant because I had said that a memorial library could be useful. How could I have just done that? I expect that some people probably would have actually gone through those few feelings as the "speakers" kept on shooting us down, by telling us we had no control. It did get me thinking, though by the end, almost like they had brainwashed me. I actually thought, "maybe a factory wouldn't be so bad, if we were helped to relocate and rebuild our businesses, if there was a Holocaust Library to teach people of our suffering, so as not to repeat itself in the future."

Reggie

Reflection

The students in Nancy's class are not labelled "gifted," but they talk and write with skill and passion. I want to stay in this classroom, not only as an observer, but as part of the collective and individual storying that continues on inside and outside the drama. The students write, the teacher writes, and I write—all of us attempting to make sense of our experiences, constructing our personal world views, changing at the very moment of writing down our thoughts, and continuing to change from the shock of reading what we have written.

Language is that which makes us human, and we are caught inside our own words, struggling to understand why we have said what we have said.

Structuring the Drama through Student Knowledge

The most valuable resource in building drama is the knowledge our students possess. If we prepare for our dramatic experiences by having the students engage in inquiries and research on the topic or issue, the data, the images, and the opinions they collect can add to the context of the improvised work, giving strength to their discussion, and allowing them to be the experts, the authorities, as they feed their information into the drama process. Similarly, if we choose an area of the curriculum they are studying as the basis for the drama work, then their study and research are given value as they use their learning within the imagined context of the drama. The students inform the drama, and the drama is enriched and deepened for the students.

Chapter 10: Helping Students Make Art and Life Connections

Drama can be either taught as a subject on the timetable or used as a learning medium in various areas of the curriculum, such as language arts, social sciences, physical education, music, or visual art. Role playing allows students to experience some of the physical and emotional aspects of any topic, and can deepen students' understanding of course content. Understanding of group organization and dynamics, as well as skill in interpersonal relationships, can be reinforced through drama. Art, music, and drama together form a powerful combination that can ignite perception and thought. Many aspects of a physical education program can reinforce and are reinforced by drama.

Exploring Art's Transformative Power

In his short novel, *The Monument*, Gary Paulsen tells the story of an artist commissioned by a small town in Middle America to create a memorial for their war dead, lost in Vietnam. As he studies the town and its people, he begins to incorporate their values into his sketches: his art reflects the townsfolk who find a shocking awareness of themselves, resulting in the tensions that drive the story to its moving conclusion.

Paulsen speaks to us about the nature of art, its form and function, and its effect on both artist and audience. "I want to show art," he says, "show how it can shake and crumble thinking, how it can bring joy and sadness at the same time, how it can own and be owned, sweep through lives and change them." Of course, this is story drama's function as well, an art form that, in Dorothy Heathcote's words, "surprises the children into knowing" what they had not suspected they could ever know, that alters their classroom lives and seeps into their collective unconscious.

Each drama group working with *The Monument* constructs its own story, drawing from the ghosts Paulsen let loose in his story. The class dynamic, the social context of the group, the past experiences in drama and narrative, the strengths of the teacher—these are the factors that affect the story drama, that create with us and for us the imaginary garden that the poet Marianne Moore talks about, "the imaginary garden with real toads," that we enter together.

Entwined in Gary Paulsen's story is my story as teacher: the struggle to create a construct that will draw into it the students' ideas and values, while, at the same time, illuminating and reflecting back what they have collectively created, so that the meaning-making experience of drama can continue on into their lives.

Demonstration: One Group's Journey—Seeking Illumination

This lesson is explored more fully in "Story Drama: Linking Narrative and Role Playing," which appears in *Children and Drama*, Third edition, by Nellie McCaslin.

Memorial, a picture book by Gary Crew and Shaun Tan, is based on a monument to the soldiers and works well with Paulsen's book, *The Monument.* Other useful picture books that handle post-war issues carefully include *The Conquerors* by David McKee, *Potatoes, Potatoes* by Anita Lobel, and *The War* by Anais Vaugelade.

A group of elementary students found some frustration and discomfort in working with the issues in Paulsen's book, but their struggle resulted in a deeper understanding of their own values and of history's complicated truths. Since I was working with students I did not know and the students had not heard or read the novel, we began as a large group discussing commemorative memorials they had seen in their own community or on holiday trips. The ensuing list was large and included fountains, statues, obelisks, and walls.

I began the drama with a problem-solving situation that paralleled the central issue of the story. The students, in small groups, were asked to role-play artists vying for a contract to create a war memorial for a small town that had lost six citizens in the Vietnam War. In role as mayor, I explained the conditions for the awarding of the contract. I then distributed large sheets of newsprint and markers for the creative planning sessions. Because the classroom teacher had persevered with co-operative learning activities, the students quickly entered the situation, and diagrammed and represented what they felt to be appropriate models for the memorial.

To help the youngsters commit to their roles, we increased the formality of the presentations by arranging a table for groups of artists in front of the townspeople. In role as mayor, I added a new tension to the proceedings by informing the artists of the benefactor's demands: the monument would be dedicated to his son who had died in the war and must represent him in full battle dress, armed for the fight. This concept grew from my observation of the groups, as I realized they had rejected any reference to weapons or military equipment.

The students wanted to build a monument to peace, but as a drama and literacy teacher, I needed to help them come to grips with the feelings of those townsfolk who had lost family members and needed to grieve. In the developing work, the students would fight long and hard to have no memorial that glorified this complicated and sad time. At the same time, I felt that I owed them a "remove" from their lives, so that through their drama work, they might come to understand the positions in which others found themselves, and in doing so, find their own lives illuminated through their art.

Because this tension of the benefactor was added after the initial planning, the groups of artists requested more time to rethink their designs. The discussions that followed were spirited, even argumentative, but were contained by the framework of the role-playing situation. As teacher, I was able to work with the small groups as a side-coach, questioning and offering encouragement.

Each group of artists began to incorporate the conditions imposed on the monument, but without sacrificing their beliefs in representing peace. They brought forward designs that included abstract monuments of the lost soldier, the spirit of war, fountains in the shape of raised hands signifying community while weapons lay under them, or peace gardens where the soldier welcomed visitors with the open arms of an unarmed guard holding birds of peace.

And yet drama thrives on incongruity, on parts of the whole lacking balance. The benefactor was always offstage, allowing the mayor to relay his response to each group's presentation and to push for an artistic representation of the soldier son in full battle regalia. Then, in this particular drama event, a youngster in role informed the mayor

> Death in war takes many lives: nurses, doctors, reporters, children, citizens, and soldiers. All lives matter, not just those who are armed. Why can't this monument stand for all the lives lost, so that the man's son will be part of this whole community that we want to remember? His spirit will be caught inside the memorial so that all of us can remember.

The students knew this eloquent response signalled a turn of events, and so the groups of artists met once more to prepare their designs. Interestingly, many began to incorporate aspects of each other's, resulting in the class members building towards a consensus of what the monument should be: a wading pool for babies, surrounded by trees and benches where parents could watch and protect and where the students could play together without fear from outside forces. And in the middle of the pool would be a young man packing his kit, preparing to leave home, to leave the circle of his village. This would be the memorial to stand alongside the one created by the novelist.

Reflection

The story of the artist/outsider has formed the basis for many role-playing lessons. In one, a group in role as Vietnamese Americans wanted the monument torn down because of war memories; in another, townspeople re-created moments in the soldier's life before he went to war; in another, tourists were found desecrating the monument and had to interview those who had created it as part of their punishment; and in a fourth, the ghosts of the war dead gathered together to express their feelings about the controversy. On each occasion, the story belonged to the tellers, and I, as teacher-editor-artist, was responsible for helping to shape it, to develop a frame that allowed it to be heard and felt by others.

Gary Paulsen's own destination for his story journey takes us to another garden where families can remember lost loved ones together:

> Trees. I thought, all this time he was coming to this he wants to make a monument with trees.
> "It should be a place to think," Mick continued. "A place to remember the men who have died."
> He went to the blackboard and began sketching in white chalk. "Here. Eighteen men have died from this area so here and here we plant trees, eighteen trees in two rows of nine in front of the courthouse on the lawn so that they make a shaded area and in the area we put seats, stone seats here and here and here so people can come and sit in the quiet shade and think of what the trees represent."
> He stopped, took a breath, and waited. All this time, the room had been quiet and it was Harley who broke the silence. "There's a place there, by the courthouse, an empty place. What's that for?"

The difficulty for the teacher of drama, as for the director of a play, is to recognize the moment when the belief is deepest. The participants come to realize the significance that underpins their work and feel satisfied that they have struggled towards a resolution that somehow honors their beliefs and illuminates their efforts.

Mick pointed to the spot with the chalk. "For the future, it may be that you will want to plant more trees there."

Another quiet time, longer than before. I could hear the clock from all the way out in the hallway ticking.

"Could we"—a quiet, almost whispered man's voice cut the silence—"name them? Could we have a small plaque on each tree naming the one the tree is for?"

I turned and saw that it was Mr. Takern and remembered that he had a son killed in Vietnam.

"The name would mean so much," he said. "The names in Washington mean so much."

Mick nodded. "We can do anything you want."

Mrs. Takern stood suddenly from where she'd been sitting on a bench next to her husband and left the room, and I could see that she was crying, holding a hanky to her face. I wondered what her son's name had been and how he had died.

"Anything you want," Mick said again. "Do we need to vote?"

This time nobody made a sound, and I knew that Mick had done it, had made the kind of monument he wanted to make for Bolton, the kind that Bolton truly wanted and just needed to be shown.

Trees.

The ending to this story touches me deeply, for both the author and the fictional artist found the truth of the tale. Therein lies the complexity of working in story drama as teacher. I must honor the ideas that the students develop, and yet I must try to structure the work so they enter the drama more deeply than they ever thought they could. Gavin Bolton describes each of us as a "teacher-artist," and that is the best definition I have discovered for picturing our work. The strength of the teacher is backed by the power of the artist in shaping the collaborative creation of 30 youngsters so that, in the end, everyone feels a sense of satisfaction from the work.

Demonstration: Struggling Ghosts, Engaged Students—Exploring Duality of Roles

In *Tales from Gold Mountain*, author Paul Yee has achieved a remarkable goal: the blending of Chinese folktales with the historical incidents of the immigration to North America of Chinese men to work on the building of the national railway and in the gold rush of the north. These stories hold the spirits of students in the strangest of ways. I want to explore each one in drama and try to discover the secrets Yee has buried in his tellings. Certainly the weaving of folklore and historical incidents offers us, as teachers, dozens of universal truths that can be tapped into for dramatic exploration.

One Grade 8 class listened to me tell the ghost tale of Rider Chan, in which a young man carries messages, gold, and medicine to workers during the Gold Rush. As Chan crosses a river, his leg is grabbed by a ghost. It is released only when Chan agrees to bury the corpses of dead workers lost in the river, so that they may have eternal rest. The situation of the

Author Paul Yee has written several books incorporating the legends that Chinese workers brought to the New World:

Tales from Gold Mountain
Dead Man's Gold and Other Stories
Ghost Train

The Rainbow People, by Laurence Yep, is also built around these tales.

ghosts in the river represents the very stuff of drama: students can rise from the floor, moving ghost-like towards the rider on shore, entreating the living one to help them. The drama offers the opportunity to explore the duality of roles: the ghosts negotiating with the living and the students attempting to convince Chan, in this case me, the teacher, working in role. The students, excellent at argument, were logical thinkers used to debate and to winning.

The students formed small groups in role as ghosts, to plan strategies for convincing Chan to bury them and then return their dust to China. Gradually, their ideas turned towards a son's devotion to his mother and to the respect his culture demonstrated towards the memory of loved ones lost. When, as a class, they then positioned themselves as if in the river, speaking to the living on shore, their words evidenced a passionate attempt to move the heart of Chan. They regrouped several times to draw up new arguments, new ways of reaching the young man.

It was not until the students themselves felt the frustration and the need to change Chan's mind that the drama began to happen. They were no longer merely students play-acting in a classroom—they were in a river struggling to get out. Their language altered; they chose their words carefully, adding the weight of feeling; they used their arms, their bodies to supplement their cries of anguish; they had become a more compact group physically, standing shoulder to shoulder; they were coming to grips with the power of theatre, knowing how to effect change in others through their roles, using voice and stance and presence in order to persuade. And when I agreed to the plan of ritual burial, they felt satisfaction both inside the drama as the ghosts in pain, and outside the drama as students who had met the artistic and moral challenge presented by a teacher.

Reflection

Later, when I had read two other selections from Yee's book of tales to the class, the questions about the time period grew along with suggestions for new drama work, generated by the story and by the students' concerns about the Chinese workers. This lesson, then, could serve as the beginning for extended playmaking, depicting life in North America for Chinese workers.

Several students sent me poems reflecting upon their story work that day, showing how they had expanded their understanding of the original story through their dramatization of it. Here is one of the poems.

> *Remember*
>
> *Remember all my thoughts, my words*
> *For I am gone now, like a bird.*
> *My body rests underground, but*
> *My spirit ventures somewhere sound.*
> *Everything I did and said*
> *Recalled upon my own deathbed.*
> *Just for now I want to say,*
> *"Look at me where I lay."*

In my eyes do you see
Anything resembling me?
Now I leave you with no word
For I am gone now, like a bird.

Melanie

Demonstration: From Child's Play to Drama—Deepening Connections

In the following case, the connection between the play of the young child and the drama experience of schoolchildren was evident from the first moment the children entered the room. The class was composed of 25 boys, aged five and six years, attending a summer camp within a school setting. I had chosen another tale by Paul Yee, but rather than read aloud "Spirits of the Railway," I had asked a group of teachers on-course the day before to prepare to tell the tale as an ensemble, weaving the story around the children, and making use of a parachute to draw everyone physically inside the story circle. After listening to the story, the boys retold it to me as we sat together in a large bay window area. One teacher later wrote:

Gordon Wells and Karen Hume chronicle and analyse a similar lesson I taught to a Grade 8 class in an article, "Making Lives Meaningful: Extending Perspectives through Role Play," in *Building Moral Communities through Educational Drama*, edited by Betty Jane Wagner.

> David did not read the story. Instead, the adults in the class became group storytellers, sharing the story in role, and using a parachute to gather the children around. The parachute was a powerful symbol. Amazingly enough, the boys retained all of the information from the storytelling. This came as a surprise to me.
>
> The joy of the story and its telling! So spontaneous, so supportive of teacher for teacher and teacher for child. The children clutching the parachute, just the joy of pulling the parachute up and down delighted the children as it became a mountain, or waves, or a covering. It felt good. It gave us all something to cling to in tentative beginnings and something to soar with as we sailed through the story. I loved the storytelling and when in discussion found the use of the parachute to be spontaneous and delighted in it even more. The work happened and was allowed to happen through careful planning and then letting go. We should all "let go" and enjoy the parachutes more!

In role as railway workers, the children sat in a large circle, preparing to leave for the New World. We passed around chunks of bread, as a symbol of our memories of home life, and I narrated some of the problems ahead of us. Each child said goodbye to their families.

More and more, I find it is the students who determine the lesson, revealing to me which points are significant and which characters should come to the forefront, so that they can own the work. I construct the lesson, but they create the drama.

> The bread was significant. Almost eating part of this imaginary world. Bread, a bonding agent. I was afraid the bread would distract them but it didn't. The beauty of the bread was that it wasn't Oreo cookies. What is more communal than breaking bread? So valuable a bonding experience.
>
> There was this magnificent moment that helped me to understand the beauty of this method of teaching/creating dramas. Ben, my son in the drama, was packing to go to the new world. We finished packing and

words were welling up inside of him and he was looking directly into my eyes. I waited for him to speak and he didn't at first. Gently, I asked him if he had something to say and he pulled these words up from his soul and simply said, "I'm going." He delivered those two words so meaningfully and powerfully. He seemed to understand the significance of this decision to leave his mother and go to a strange land. I will never forget that moment.

In role as the captain, I called for volunteers to sign up for the long voyage from China to North America, offering jobs, shoes, and gold nuggets to all those who were accepted for the journey. The boys signed their names on the ship's registry, and the story drama began.

At one point, early in the session, the boys were lined up in front of David who was in role as the ship captain. They broke out into a chant of "I'm looking at you!" [apparently a familiar camp song]. David just let this run its course—a clear example of play—then went on to adding tension to deepen their belief in the drama: "Sign up and get your gold nugget!" David announced. The very process of signing their names on the yellow pad of paper by each of the children in role deepened their work.

I really liked David's question: "Is anyone in this group strong enough to remember the message of his father's ghost?" Almost all of the boys raised their hands, and this was a prelude of the drama work to come. The challenge was to get this group of boys to believe in the drama, to "be" serious mine workers, or, in other words, to move from play to dramatic play to drama.

Using a scene from the story about workers who would not enter a mine because of ghost voices, I set up the situation where the children as miners would persuade the teachers as reluctant workers to enter the tunnel; then, in the next scene, the boys in role slept in their bunks and the teachers as spirits whispered words of advice to them concerning the dangers of entering the mine.

As a class, the children shared their stories from the night visitors together, and the drama grew from the need to give all of the bodies of those killed in the mine disaster a decent burial. I asked the teachers to lie quietly on the floor while all the children gently covered them with the parachute.

For these boys the aesthetic moment (and what a moment it was!) came at the end of the drama when they symbolically buried the adults with the parachute. They believed in what they were doing.

The work ended as the children bowed three times to the mine leader, and the story drama was complete.

Reflection

These children seemed too young for such extended, focused drama, and I brought into the lesson as much dramatic play as I could. I was thankful for the parachute, the bread, and the teachers who followed my lead like the most sensitive of ensemble players, foregoing their own directorial urges, and helping me to find within those pure childhood hearts the fragile moments of collective playmaking. I shall never forget the burial. The children should not have been able to do that, but they did. They gave us more than we deserved.

> I think of them [the little boys], after the fact, and realize they have helped me see her [my daughter] in a new light, and I see them through the vision of Aurelia. As I think of her, it begins to dawn on me what they are ... the instant of being brilliant beyond years, on the edge of tears, lunging forward into laughter at the turn of a thought, the depths, the strangely wonderful and unique humor, the single-mindedness and determination to stick to their guns, right or wrong, mixed with a deep desire to please me for the sake of pleasing me ... the sheer delight of being six.

Demonstration: The Porcelain Plate—Delving into the Human Heart

I find every story by Richard Kennedy full of twists and turns. Students can respond with their own suggestions to the complicated and fantastical plots in *Richard Kennedy: Collected Stories.*

"Where do you get your ideas?" They come from memories, images, dreams, story happenings, but in truth, I get ideas because I look for ideas ... I wondered about Humpty Dumpty one day. If he had been put back together by all the King's Horses and all the King's Men, could they ever have done it right? And if not—what? Also, after fourteen years of marriage, I was alone, my wife and children elsewhere. Broken up.

Richard Kennedy

I first read "The Porcelain Man" as a picture book, and when I subsequently found it in *Richard Kennedy: Collected Stories*, I realized that it was part of a significant body of work by a fine American writer. I first heard the story told by my friend Bob Barton, a master storyteller. Now, whenever I read this narrative aloud, I hear Bob's voice whispering in my ear.

In this startling story of loneliness and love, author Richard Kennedy takes us into a fantasy that results in our seeing deeper into the human heart. A lonely girl living with her nasty father comes to build a man of porcelain, who tells her that he loves her. The twists and turns help us realize the difficulty of living with our choices in life. Eventually, the porcelain man is shattered, and his remains become a set of dishes. The story ends with the girl marrying another man, but at dinner, her porcelain plate says, "I love you."

With a group of 15 girls attending a summer camp, I began by reading "The Porcelain Man" as they sat in a semi-circle, with the teachers behind them looking on. In the ensuing discussion, the children were hesitant to participate, and I struggled with a variety of questions, trying to find an entry point into the drama. I wanted to keep the group working as an ensemble. Eventually, we explored different thoughts about the talking plate, drawn from our memories of the story.

I presented a problem: the girls, in role as new brides, had to decide whether to sell or hide from their new husbands the dishes that could speak of love. Each girl discussed her views with one of the teachers who had been observing, now acting as a confidante. I role-played the husband, and asked the girls, one by one, in role as wife, to tell me about the porcelain dishes that seemed so special to her. The girls then demonstrated their different approaches to the problem, from obliterating the porcelain plates to guarding them as hope for their future.

Some of the teachers worked in role as well, as neighbors who had borrowed the plate or as villagers who had heard stories from those who knew the girl from her past. One teacher wrote:

Now David was ready to begin role playing as the husband, and tension was added by David in making the role of the husband harsh and narrow-minded. This tension helped the girls begin to believe in the drama.

What stands out the most in my mind was my young partner's belief that if her new husband found out that the plate loved her, he would be crushed. The statement said so much to me. She understood the difference between a husband and a father, which many of the girls seemed not to understand. She was committed to protecting her husband. And the use of the word "crushed" gave me an image that she believed her husband was as fragile as the porcelain man.

To deepen the awareness of the dilemma, I explained that the husband had been called to war, and in role as husband, I asked each of the girls in the circle, as my wife, to create a special meal on the porcelain plate to take with me. I had focused on the one plate from the set that had demonstrated the ability to say, "I love you." How would each girl respond to my request to take the plate with me?

Discussion brought out a range of possibilities that reflected some deep thinking and problem solving. A "light bulb" moment for one of the girls was her suggestion to break the plate, mix it with other pieces of porcelain, and make two plates, one for him and one she could keep.

These wonderful beings came to us, in role, to debate the pros and cons of whether to keep the plate or give it to their husband. Stephanie is a very bright, verbal, independent young lady. I struggled to suppress my views of what she should do, resorting to comments and questions to find out how she felt in her heart. I found it fascinating, listening to her point of view since it was quite different from mine. Yes, she loved her husband, but she would not give up the plate. It had a special meaning to her, and she feared her husband would not understand. She could not put into words what this "special meaning" was, but from the look in her eyes, it was important and exciting to have something of their own. For a moment, I wondered, "Is this the age little girls have diaries and begin to lock them?" She liked sticking to her guns and being in Opposition to her husband. Later, when in role, David asked her, "Do you know where the plate is?" she replied with a great deal of strength, "I broke it and didn't save the pieces."

The range of response from all the girls to this question revealed as much. "I'm not going to give it to you!" "I can't give it to you. I think it might be . . ." "I'll look in the kitchen." "The plate is in the brook!" "I borrowed it." "And she broke it." Some were so strong and spoke out. For example, when the girl said, "I have it but I won't give it to you." Some felt strongly but had no voice. A little blonde girl, who had not spoken much, spontaneously mouthed, "My father gave it to me," to no one in particular while a stronger student was speaking out. I had not made that connection until I read her lips. The father had given the daughter the makings of the porcelain man.

The students worked in small groups, along with the teachers, to create silent, still-image scenes symbolic of the story. Then, to draw the session to a close, I returned to the opening scene. The students formed a circle with a teacher standing behind each girl, hands on shoulders, as an adviser, whispering suggestions and support. I interviewed the girls each of whom was in role as the wife about whether they would choose to keep the plate in their new homes. While the teachers advised, the students responded with their own heartfelt ideas, often in contradiction to their advisers.

> David told us [the adults] that his goal in drama work is to reach an aesthetic moment that the children create, that they are in charge of. To me, this final moment in the drama with these girls was where it happened.

Reflection

These girls had formed their relationships before I had arrived in the school. Many of the teachers were greeted affectionately with hugs and kisses, and I knew that throughout the work, I would be the alien. Working in role as a catalyst was the first choice I made, and the students' ideas demonstrated intense thought and extreme confidence.

Making choices is what I do as a teacher, and the dynamics of the students, the space, and the function of the lesson all drive me towards the rhythm of the work. Each teacher selects from a menu hidden deep within, and as we watch others making choices, we add to our own storehouse, knowing all the while we will never follow that schema again. Such is the unique quality of each teaching experience.

So many concerns arose, and some of them still haunt me. When there are such powerful audiences for theatre, extravagant auditoria with computerized lighting boards, companies and artists around the world sharing their talents, 50 years of drama educators nurturing and extending the techniques of the teachers, how will we, as classroom teachers, remember to listen to the tiniest children's voices hidden in the corners, to work with those young people who will never be "on stage," to deepen the talents of those who feel they do not even need us?

Like children's books that exist only when a child is present, we only truly teach when the art and the child connect, so that for the moment, each of us, child and teacher, belongs to the "what if" world.

Dear Mr. Booth:

Thank you for coming and showing us that drama. I really enjoyed it! I thought that drama was only where you do plays, but you showed me that there are different kinds of drama. It was really good!

Yours truly,
Jamie

Chapter 11: Sharing Story Dramas as Actors and as Audience

I was visiting my brother Jack's Grade 8 class in June on the last day of school. After the children had been dismissed, a girl returned to the room, went to her desk at the back, walked over to us carrying an imaginary object, and said in a soft voice to my brother, "I'd forgotten my mixing bowl from the village. Thank you." She had needed to tell her teacher of the importance of that lesson conducted in a long-ago January, when she had been allowed to be a woman in a tribe, a woman who had cast the vote determining if they would leave the area for a new home. The group did move on, and she had chosen to carry her bowl. Now she was giving it back to her teacher.

Sharing our drama creations is an important aspect of the art of theatre. In its widest sense, theatre is communal; those who are acting are integral to the meaning-making experiences of those who are observing. At the same time, those acting grow and change because of the responses of those who are audience. As teachers, we need to provide meaningful contexts for supporting honest presentations—having seven-year-olds shouting on stage before 400 parents may not be the best setting for growing through drama.

In one example of a meaningful context, the teacher of a senior drama class in a secondary school wanted to share a production with an elementary class. Together, we worked out a co-operative drama venture. The high school students researched information from the Internet about the habits and behaviors of coyotes, and then built stories—myths actually—about the coyote culture, weaving the data into first person lore that would be shared in the rituals of the coyote people. The work of the young people was deep and sensitive, and the stories connected to the folklore surrounding these creatures.

The presentation was unusual in form: the students arrived at the school where I had been working with a second grade class on the "coyote trap" drama for two days (see Chapter 7). I instructed the primary students to lie on the floor as journalists, tired from interviewing and writing about the farmers and their problems. They were to close their eyes and dream about the coyotes. In the quiet of the room, the high school students crept in, and one on one, whispered their mythic stories in the ears of the students lying quietly in the floor. When they were finished, these students left quietly, and I asked the students as journalists to wake and open their eyes. Perhaps their responses were the most fascinating of all the dramas I have been involved in.

The primary students spoke as if they had indeed dreamed the entire visit:

"I think I had a dream and went to coyote land where they told me stories."

"This coyote told me about how he hunted and found food, and I think I was with him while he hunted."

"My coyote said that we were special and could help them live and I heard her and I want to tell the farmers."

The stories went on and on, and I am not sure if the students were able to separate the drama and the dreams, but when I reflected later with the secondary students, they felt excited about the sharing of their explorations. Research and playmaking had combined to create an unusual and powerful theatre moment in the lives of both the high school and primary students.

As this experience suggests, there are many ways of presenting creative work to outside audiences. Typically, in story drama, groups can share their work. When all the groups have shaped their contributions, each can present their ideas in turn. But first, we can decide on how the other groups fit into the work as role-playing spectators. For example, perhaps each group is presenting its interpretation of a crime. Those watching can role-play townspeople and decide which interpretation they think works best. They can then—like a jury—decide on the guilt of an individual.

The Relationship between Participants and Spectators

See *How Theatre Educates: Convergences and Counterpoints with Artists, Scholars, and Advocates*, edited by Kathleen Gallagher and David Booth.

The definition of drama in school has broadened considerably. At one time, it was equated with "stage" presentations—a performance at a school assembly or a parents' night, or a play put on by a visiting group. Today, though, drama in education encompasses many kinds of activities, from Kindergarten children's play in a dress-up centre to a professional touring company's presentation of a play specially written for young audiences.

The Drama in Education Continuum

exploring   sharing   playmaking   presenting   performing

⟶

Participant ⟵————————————————— Spectator

Each class's needs will help you determine when and what to show others.

Exploring drama

The goal of the drama lesson is to explore ideas, roles, physical and verbal interaction, feelings, and attitudes. Just as in art class, the goal is not the showing of the work. There may be reasons for sharing, but exploration and learning come first.

Sharing drama

Sharing is the interaction that occurs when individuals or groups communicate with others. In classroom work, those watching can see different interpretations of the text; they can be part of a sequential sharing of the scenes from the story; or they can help with work in progress, as each group takes suggestions for further exploration that lead to a broader exploration of the theme for everyone involved.

127

When planning to share the work of the students with others, the effective teacher considers the following:

- the purpose for the sharing, and what impact the sharing will have on the work being explored in drama

- the social health of the group, and whether the students wish to share the work (e.g., should beginners be encouraged to show work or should they concentrate on themselves and their own group?)

- the option of exploring informal ways of working with an audience (e.g., informal demonstration for discussion or observational purposes, on-the-spot spontaneous sharing during the lesson, or sharing work with others who are on a similar exploration);

- the advantages and disadvantages of setting up situations where volunteers can do the sharing (e.g., an "after-four" group)

- the value of putting the emphasis on encouraging more exploration and development of new ideas that deepen the drama

Playmaking

Playmaking is improvisation extended into a sequence of lessons organized around creating a more formal, structured piece of work—a play. Presentation before an audience is not necessarily the goal of this activity. Playmaking enables the students to learn about dramatic structure and to experience the satisfaction of having carried a relatively ambitious project through to a conclusion. The source for the extended improvisation may be an aspect of the curriculum, a story, or suggestions from the students. The teacher focuses the drama by defining the situation and the task.

Students may wish to extend or polish the drama on another day, and this further exploration may prove beneficial. If presentation is a goal, the teacher should ensure the necessary time for development before polishing is begun.

Every drama group should do a performance project because some aspects of improvising cannot be learned in any other way. It is pointless, though, to embark on such a project until that project feels like a logical extension of work in improvising.

Presenting drama

Presenting drama involves sharing work with others who have not been engaged in the process of exploring and learning. It might involve showing the work to another class in the same school or to students working on similar activities, but at different times and places. The teachers of both the spectators and the participants need to take into account that different classes work differently and have different evaluation criteria. Drama to be presented may require some polishing and refinement, since the emotional risks to the students are greater in more formal situations.

Performing drama

Performing is a formal event, a way of sharing dramatic work with an audience that is outside the creative process, and that sees and evaluates the finished product, perhaps unaware of the process. It is important that the performance be polished and practised to help make the actors more comfortable and assured, and for the sake of what they are trying to present. If something is worth presenting publicly, the creators would want as much time as possible to develop their vision and rehearse. With children, we can minimize the tensions of performing by working with a smaller audience, using a friendlier space, such as a library, arranging to perform before supportive friends, and involving all of the children as an ensemble.

Beginning a drama club: An extracurricular club, initiated by a teacher, provides a focus for students interested in performing. The teacher's role is to help the group develop into a "team" and ensure that the activities engaged in emphasize co-operation, interdependence, the students' sensitivity to one another and to the group, and a desire to share fun as opposed to being the centre of attention. The teacher may wish to assist the group in creating a play, using as possible sources a student's suggestion, a story, a poem, a script, a character, a situation in the news, some aspect of the curriculum, music, sound improvisation, or slides.

Seeing visiting artists

Schools are wise to take advantage of programs that place practising artists in the classroom or, even better, where there can be direct involvement with the students. As a result of these visits, students and teachers can explore new methods of working in drama and often try on new ways of responding to professional artists. Students can benefit greatly from seeing performances by local artists and groups. Planned carefully, such visits can inspire follow-up activities in the school that will enrich the curriculum and extend the students' artistic experiences.

As teachers, we are responsible for preparing the student audience. We should let the students know about a performance well ahead of time and discuss all aspects of the event, such as the name of the company, the type of company (e.g., a mime group, a theatre company, an instrumental group, a dance company), and the date and time of the performance. Class work in preparation might include exploring concepts, discussing the story line, and previewing what to watch for. A study guide from the guest group, if available, can be helpful in these areas.

Various activities can also take place after the visit, for example:

- discussing the visual and aural aspects of the performance, as well as possible interpretations (*Was there a message in the story? Was there something to be learned about the world we live in? about the lives of the people portrayed?*)

- writing, perhaps a speech in role as one of the characters, thank-you letters to the company, or reviews of the play or the players' performances

- making artwork of scenes from the play, the audience at the play, a character in the play, the costumes, or the set designs

Breaking role stereotypes

Story drama leaders are wise not to have preconceived ideas about who should be the actor, who should be the audience, and who might not belong at all. This idea is powerfully reinforced by two experiences of mine, where a caretaker played an unexpected, but significant role.

When I began teaching drama, my principal's advice included the adage, "Be good to the caretaker. He'll know all your secrets and control your future." Too true. I remembered my first drama lesson as a student in eighth grade, just after World War II. Emigrants from England were forced to take jobs that they had not been trained for. The principal/teacher knew our caretaker's background in theatre, and each Thursday afternoon, we were taught movement and drama by the man who cleaned the floors and scrubbed the toilets on Monday and Tuesday. His abilities caused us to respect him no less than our teacher, and the work progressed until parents' night when we demonstrated our skeleton world, using "Danse Macabre" to help the adults see beyond our adolescent difficulties. I loved that evening; we touched on dance and drama, and it will be with me always. At the conclusion of the sharing, everyone drank Freshie and ate cookies and talked theatre, and at 10 p.m., we left, while the caretaker cleaned up after us, and was alone in his gymnasium with his broom and dustpan, alone in his theatre.

And what would our dragon play have been without another caretaker? We were conducting our drama program in a church hall, and the adults were having difficulty building belief in their own roles, inspired by tales of King Arthur's knights. It was hard for 30 adults on a hot July day to make drama happen, and as I sweated and struggled, the caretaker came into the room to ask what time we would be finished. Out of nothing but desperation, I asked him to find the truth within the dragon tapestries that had been discovered in a cave so that we could free a knight from the curse. And he stared, walked around the tableau figures, and began to tell us what he saw. He had no teeth and no drama training, but he knew the secrets of that tapestry. When the caretaker left 30 minutes later, we gathered in our reflection circle and talked about status stereotypes and strangers entering our drama.

Dynamic Forms of Presentation

In helping us find structures for building and presenting our drama work, the theatre world offers us several different frameworks for both exploring a particular theme and for organizing experiences into a coherent whole for an audience to understand and appreciate. Rather than follow a direct narrative in developing the drama work, we can explore a variety of selections with different strategies and then use one of these frameworks to tie the separate bits and pieces together.

The following modes, described in more detail below, can be useful in building drama units that can then be shared with an audience:

- anthology presentations
- docudramas
- Ensemble Drama

Developing an Anthology Presentation

An anthology is a dramatization of several selections representing a variety of material—poems, stories, events, excerpts from novels, articles, and songs. Here is an outline for experimenting with an anthology presentation:

1. The class decides on the theme that they wish to explore dramatically. This theme can be general, such as hate or love, or specific, such as why people fight. If the theme is general, it usually becomes more specific as the class decides which aspects of the theme they are most interested in. It is important to remember that choosing a theme is extremely difficult and demands full discussion by all members of the group. There is little point in attempting to create something to which everyone is not committed.

2. After the theme is chosen, each group member is responsible for finding and bringing in material that relates to the theme in some significant way. This material can be drawn from a wide range of sources.

3. The group next examines, discusses, and analyses this material, retaining those things which it considers dramatically effective and setting aside anything that does not fit the theme. Choice of material will depend on the length of the anthology, which can be anywhere from 10 minutes to a couple of hours.

4. After selecting the material, the group decides on an order in which to present the material.

5. Next, the group begins to work with pieces of material. It is unnecessary to work through the selections from beginning to end at this point. Rather, it is important to start interpreting the selections dramatically.

6. The next major problem is linking one selection to the next. Transitions are important because they provide continuity in the anthology. Since the presentation will not have a plot or any main characters, the focus is on showing aspects of the theme in a way that is logical or dramatically powerful. Transitions can be effectively created through movement, song, recurring statements, improvisation, or any other means which will take the audience from one scene into the next.

7. At this point in rehearsal, the group may decide that some material is unsatisfactory and will have to be changed. Also, some rearranging of material may be desired. This is perfectly normal in the creative process, and we should encourage analysis and discussion of these matters. Making an anthology is a group creative process, and the perceptions of others are invaluable in helping to make the presentation the best it can be.

8. When the order of the selections has been agreed upon, pieces have been rehearsed, and transitions have been established, it is then time to work on the beginning and ending of the presentation. An effective beginning states the theme in some way and draws the audience into the presentation. The ending should be a final statement of the group's thoughts and feelings about the theme and should leave the audience thinking about the presentation and its ideas.

Building a Docudrama

Docudrama combines the word "documentary" with the word "drama." It is the first word which distinguishes this form of presentation from other forms. The techniques of gathering, selecting, ordering, and dramatizing material are very similar to those described in the previous section, Developing an Anthology Presentation; it is the material which differentiates docudrama from anthology.

The word "documentary" implies that the material is factual and historical. It also implies that the theme or concept of the presentation is related to something that has occurred in the past (history) or something that is occurring now (current events).

Participants research material using all the resources available, perhaps libraries, museums, galleries, records offices, kits, and rare books. They may also interview people who have knowledge of, or stories about, the relevant events. Generally, a source will be one of two kinds: primary (an eyewitness account of relevant events) or secondary (an interpretation or retelling by people not present at the event). The docudrama can be based on either or both types of sources.

Once the material is collected, participants follow a process of dramatization similar to that used in anthology. The major problem that will arise is avoiding the distortion of factual information. The aim is for the dramatic interpretation to stay true to the original material.

Docudrama is a valuable dramatic technique that allows participants to assemble information on important events and issues, and examine how they think and feel about them.

Creating Ensemble Drama

Ensemble Drama provides an opportunity for a large group of students to participate in a dramatic presentation. The group, which can vary from 20 to 100 members, pools its artistic and creative responses and develops a unique, spontaneous dramatic event through the integration of drama, dance, music, and the visual arts. This spontaneity, with its blending of the various arts, can lift drama into new forms of expression.

Ensemble Drama offers participants insight into the power of ritualistic storytelling, one of the oldest forms of drama. The source material for Ensemble Drama can be drawn from many stories, including myths, legends, and folktales, which contain timeless or universal truths. The message in the story should be as relevant now as it was to the people for whom the story was originally told. Ideally, the story should have many characters, strong physical action, and direct, simple language.

After choosing a story, the group is divided into subgroups. Each subgroup is assigned a specific task. Possible subgroups include these:

- *Storytellers:* This group delivers the narrative of the story by reading, by improvisation, or by a combination of both. Note that choral speech can be used successfully here. Rehearsal of reading and storytelling is important so that members will gain dramatic power and effectiveness. As in Readers Theatre, the group can also create strong visual images by the way actors are placed in the performing area.

- *Dancers/Movement interpreters:* This group rehearses those parts of the story that can be dramatized through dance and movement. Vocalization can be added through the use of chants where appropriate.

- *Musicians:* This group provides percussion music with either real or improvised instruments for the storytelling.

- *Artists:* This group makes masks and costumes, and designs backdrops or paintings to enhance the story. During the dramatization, members provide lighting and visual effects. The artists may even wish to be part of the setting themselves.

Each group practises on its own until called to the performance area, any large open space, inside or outdoors, which has been "dressed" by the artists during the practice time.

Performance of Ensemble Drama does not require an audience because each group of participants is the audience for the other groups. The performance begins on a given cue and unfolds spontaneously. Each group is attentive to the other parts of the story. If need be, one person can be appointed director to cue each group when to begin and when to end.

Demonstration: Anthem—Making the Words Their Own

The impact of language on drama was made evident to me while working with 150 Grade 7 to Grade 13 drama students and 40 teachers in a series of drama workshops. My contribution involved a whole-group session that was to highlight a local sesquicentennial celebration theme.

In planning my structure for the work, I realized I could not simply tell the group that they should care about their history—they would have to appreciate the past inside the drama frame. After introducing the theme, I put the participants into small groups and had them prepare various aspects of it, using strategies such as choral speaking, music, and set design. Later, the groups came together in an ensemble improvisation.

The visual arts group, using tin foil, plastic sheets and lights, had changed the meeting room into a futuristic holding tank. As the other students entered the transformed space, they were in the setting for the drama. In role, I explained that they were to be held prisoner here until all vestiges of national history had been "wiped from the slate," so that the society of the future would hold no prejudices or past allegiances, and we could begin to build a new and totally free nation.

As the drama work grew, the language changed most drastically. One student's summary describes her perceptions of the experience.

> *"No! Not the treatment!" cried one of the bolder prisoners in mock terror. Such idle threats could not intimidate us. Instantly the merciless jail warden spotted his prey and silenced him with one fell swoop of cross-examination. Some were overpowered by his strength, but others stood their ground. Our heritage was on trial.*
>
> *I had the privilege of being a prisoner for an afternoon. The atmosphere was so intense and unified that we burst into singing, an effort to overwhelm the judge. The improvisation ended nicely when two prisoners stood up and led us in the singing of "O Canada" in role. For once the anthem meant much more to me than a minute and a half of regulated morning exercises. It was a satisfying conclusion to a long and interesting day of creative sharing.*
>
> Drama student

Reflection

The student had seen herself and others shift attitudes, and the quality of the language was the indicator. She begins her account by stating that the comments at the beginning of the lesson were made in "mock terror," and I concur. The older students required much more time to accept the artifice of the situation and to suspend disbelief. But as the action moved on, the tone, the syntax, the volume of the comments began to alter. The participants' arguments deepened as their language strengthened, driven by the emotion of the moment.

The students resented and resisted the implication that history was of no importance. As I in role hammered at the elimination of all history, they, in turn, fought passionately against me in defence of keeping what they felt was theirs. And in the end they prevailed. I concluded the drama after they sang "O Canada."

The participants had moved to using the words of others—the lyrics of an anthem—as support for their struggle. But they had made those words their own.

After a presentation, regardless of the formal or informal dynamic, students will have so much to share with one another about their experiences as actors and the responses of their audience. We need to establish effective modes for their reactions to the public sharing of their ideas—journals, small-group discussions, further rehearsals, or even select scenes to be explored in different ways. It may be helpful to have members of the audience contribute to the discussion in carefully set-up groups, so that they can discuss the issues of the drama as well as the qualities of the performance. Our goal in working with students is always to deepen the learning, not necessarily to provide critiques.

Chapter 12: Assessing Learning from Story Drama

The practical assessment of students taking part in drama activities is not without problems; indeed, it poses challenges.

Challenges in Assessing Drama Experiences

The various types of learning that occur in a drama program do not lend themselves equally well to the assessment process. In drama, the teacher assesses both the growth of inner experience and the public form of the representation of thought and feeling. Even though drama is a shared activity, individuals and their development are of fundamental importance.

When it comes to assessment, the teacher has much to consider. Cognitive, affective, and (at times) psychomotor learning occur simultaneously, making it difficult for the teacher to assess all the information that indicates learning in drama. A further difficulty is that assessment often needs to take place while the activities are in progress.

A drama experience is more than the sum of its parts. It requires an empathetic response from the teacher as well as an assessment of what has been learned. For example, the teacher could assess the drama of the class on the basis of the insights that have been gained, the extending and elaboration of language that have occurred, or the new understanding that a group has reached. If the teacher's intent in drama is to deepen the students' thinking, the impact of the work can be determined from their reactions. Their degree of involvement can be examined through the quality of their discussion, the intensity of their absorption in and awareness of role, and their range of language. An appreciation of the drama's outcome by the students—their ability to see the consequence of events—should also be recorded.

Demonstration: Of Skins Left on the Shore—Observing the Work

Drama work, although it did not take place at set times, had been a major part of a three-week literature unit centred on the myths, poems, and stories of selchies, mermaids, and mermen. The activities had been stimulated by the junior students' reading; I as teacher had shaped these activities so that a variety of drama strategies could be used and a range of assessments made possible.

The story of the changelings has been a theme of several books that work effectively as drama sources:

Greyling by Jane Yolen
The Selkie Girl by Susan Cooper
The Seal Mother by Mordecai Gerstein
The Boy Who Lived with the Seals by Rafe Martin and David Shannon
The Music of Dolphins by Karen Hesse
The Old Country by Mordecai Gerstein

In the old tale, beautiful seal-women leave their skins on the shore while they sing and swim in the sea. A man, infatuated with them, steals one of the skins, and the seal-woman whose skin it is, is forced to stay with him on shore for many years, bearing him children. Finally, one day, she finds the skin and disappears back into the sea forever. The powerful story tells of transformation, spiritual as well as physical, loss as well as gain, heartbreak as well as love. From my readings of picture books, the class I was working with had heard several versions of the tale.

During each session, we explored various aspects of the legend, and the student teachers and I began to collect data from observations both while inside the activities and while distanced from the work as observers. By using this information, the teachers could develop a profile of assessment for each child, for the class as a community, and for the teaching program itself.

The following record lists the strategies used in our work, the variety of activities that took place, and the assessment observations drawn from the teaching.

Strategy	Activity	Assessment
Responding to a story in role	Working with *Greying*, a story by Jane Yolen, the students created the village where a seal-boy lived.	Committing themselves to role Building an environment Identifying with drama context
Exploring ideas alone and unobserved	Each child, at the same time but working alone, explored the process of changing from a sea creature into a human.	Developing a character Working autonomously Accepting a role
Improvising in groups	Each group created a scene where a selchie was first seen by villagers.	Moving in and out of role Selecting and evaluating appropriately from the possibilities Taking risks
Taking a role in an interview	In each group, one reporter interviewed three villagers about sightings of sea people.	Taking part in small-group work Drawing on a variety of indirect experiences Engaging in the drama Revealing feelings in role
Reporting on events	Each reporter described the interview to the villager to see if there were inaccuracies.	Reflecting on activity Making use of space Having a sense of audience Responding to ideas of others

Strategy	Activity	Assessment
Depicting through group tableaux	The students retold the story by creating six group tableaux that depicted the incidents.	Sharing, valuing, and responding to others Connecting ideas Staying on task
Choral speaking and chanting	The villagers created a chant to call for help in ridding the village of sea creatures.	Interpreting text Having common artistic intentions Reflecting upon emotional response
Interpreting and reading aloud	The class was divided into groups to work on sections of a story. They used the convention of Readers Theatre to interpret and retell the tale.	Interpreting the words of others Collaborating and co-operating with others Supporting the contributions of others
Play-making as a class: Sharing and appreciating a presentation	The class created a version of the story, built from their explorations in role, and shared it with students in a younger grade.	Shaping the work artistically Establishing common artistic purposes Gaining an overview of the work Employing different functions of language
Mapping and graphing in role	The students mapped out the island where the villagers lived, indicating the areas inhabited by sea creatures.	Reflecting on and reworking the drama Recognizing implications of actions Hypothesizing and brainstorming
Making masks and storytelling	The students created masks of the sea people to wear in the final ritual of storytelling as a village.	Understanding the art form Using various drama crafts Revealing awareness of dynamic of audience
Singing in role	The class learned the Selchie Song from the text and sang it.	Growing as and in an ensemble Interpreting print sensitively Maintaining mood

Strategy	Activity	Assessment
Exploring through sound and dance drama	The students created the sounds of the sea people to accompany a dance drama of a sea changeling being forced to leave the village against his will.	Creating a dramatic context Working as part of an ensemble Identifying with concerns of drama
Exploring with mime	The students mimed putting on and taking off sealskins each day, and hiding them from humans.	Exploring and communicating non-verbally Investigating possibilities Viewing self as part of ensemble
Doing games and exercises	The class played "The Hidden Key" (a game where blindfolded players catch another player who attempts to steal a key), as a prelude to the story of the changeling.	Co-operating through play Working without teacher intervention Interacting positively with others

Reflection

In this drama lesson, the students also used the Role on the Wall strategy: they represented in picture form information necessary as the drama progressed. They traced each other's bodies on brown paper and then cut the tracings out. The figures formed skins that we first displayed, then put into a pile, rolled up, bound with elastic, and hid. Suddenly, the students' roles were distanced, but in a way, the selchie quality was heightened. These skins were symbols of the drama and of the tension that lay at its heart.

One of the main goals in drama is to have our students learn to reflect "in action," to alter what they are saying or doing in order to enter the drama work more fully or with more authenticity. This distancing is the art of creating drama—the student is both spectator and participant at the same time. We need to hang our other selves on the wall once in a while in order to see what is underneath.

Four Phases of Drama Assessment

All areas of learning can be observed both when the student is *in* role within the drama and *out* of role during planning, negotiating, and reflecting. For example, within the context of a game, a student can be co-operating out of role as a participant in a warm-up activity or acting in role as a member of a tribe taking part in the game as ritual.

By ongoing assessment, the teacher can design the program to meet the needs and expectations of the class. These are the four phases:

- exploring ideas and feelings through drama

- responding to the ideas and feelings of others

- communicating ideas and feelings to others

- reflecting upon the drama experience

These are presented in checklist format, "Assessing Growth in Drama," to serve as an assessment tool. See pages 140 and 141.

Assessing Growth in Drama

To observe the level of development in each phase of drama growth, you may find this checklist helpful. Although the outcomes are organized under four themes, students will be exploring many different aspects of drama in any one lesson; over time, their abilities should grow and develop in all four areas of drama learning. This checklist has been used in a variety of classroom situations.

❑ **Phase 1: Exploring Ideas and Feelings through Drama**
The students use drama as a medium for making meaning, both individually and in groups.

Does the student

    participate verbally and non-verbally?

    focus attention and energy?

    contribute ideas in and out of role?

    represent ideas and feelings using various drama modes?

    accept, develop, and extend a role?

    demonstrate engagement in the drama?

    hypothesize and investigate possibilities?

❑ **Phase 2: Responding to the Ideas and Feelings of Others**
The students interact with other members of the class in both small and large groups; through negotiating and collaborating with others within an imagined context, they make private and public meanings.

Does the student

    respond in appropriate ways?

    accept and support the contribution of others?

    work well in small and large groups?

    work with and without teacher intervention?

    take risks, adapt, and show flexibility?

    view self as part of the ensemble?

    develop role through interactive involvement?

    identify with the attitudes of the role?

    challenge ideas within the drama?

    accept teacher in role?

    use language to question, defend, persuade, interview, and elaborate?

❏ **Phase 3: Communicating Ideas and Feelings to Others**

The students use the forms of drama to communicate with others who are working in role within the drama, or who are watching the drama as an informal or formal audience.

Does the student

> use voice appropriately and effectively?
>
> use various forms of drama: gesture, mime, movement, improvisation, interpretation, storytelling?
>
> maintain an appropriate mood and atmosphere?
>
> read aloud effectively?
>
> write in role to build the drama?
>
> make use of masks, props, instruments, and costumes to enrich the drama?
>
> understand the dynamics of performance before an audience?
>
> select, shape, and present ideas and feelings?
>
> use a variety of forms of presentation?

❏ **Phase 4: Reflecting upon the Drama Experience**

The students think about the content of the drama they have created, as well as their own contributions in making that drama happen. Reflection occurs both as the drama is developing and when it has ended.

Does the student

> contribute, receive, clarify, and modify meanings?
>
> recognize the implications of the content?
>
> reveal and share insights?
>
> question the concepts within the drama?
>
> connect the drama to personal experience?
>
> contribute personal experiences to help create the drama?
>
> reflect upon the emotional response generated by the drama?
>
> reflect on the performance of visiting theatre groups?
>
> extend the drama through other modes of response—journals, art, poetry?
>
> judge and evaluate the learning?
>
> examine the form of the dramatic exploration?

Program Assessment in Drama

As teachers of drama in education, we need to constantly reassess the approaches taken to drama in our classrooms. Maintaining flexibility and a sense of exploration and discovery is vital. Our challenge is to select from a wide range of strategies to meet the needs of the curriculum, and of the class we are teaching.

Analysing a Drama Lesson

Effective assessment will tell us how or when to move students on, when to use a particular strategy, and what will enrich the drama process.

❏ Does the focus engage the students' interest?

❏ Does the program allow the students to work together in a variety of ways?

❏ Does the focus have sufficient depth so the students can imaginatively explore it in a variety of ways?

❏ Is the program building on the students' past experience?

❏ Is the classroom environment flexible enough to accommodate various ways of working?

❏ Are the students aware of the possibilities in the environment of styles of work?

❏ Does the use of the environment reflect the purpose of the students?

❏ Is the type of drama building upon and extending the students' experience of dramatic modes of working?

❏ Are the students getting access to a wide variety of types of drama?

❏ Does the type of drama complement the purpose of the drama?

❏ Does the type of drama build upon the interests and abilities of the students?

❏ Does the chosen style relate to the purpose of the drama and to the students?

❏ Are the students getting access to a variety of styles?

_____

_____

_____

_____

_____

_____

Assessing the Drama Program

A total drama program may be evaluated on the basis of the flexibilities of curriculum design.

❏ Do the program and the individual drama activities engage students within their own abilities and experience?

❏ Does the program employ a variety of focuses, organizational groupings, and ways of working?

❏ Does the program allow the students to make more and more of the choices?

❏ Does the program allow the students to reflect on both personal and shared cultural understandings?

Reflecting on a Drama Lesson

You might consider the following questions:

❏ Was the content of the drama lesson appropriate and relevant to the students' concerns?

❏ How capable are the students of assessing their own work?

❏ Did the role playing done by the teacher serve a useful purpose?

❏ Did the drama lesson stimulate lively discussion and reflection?

❏ Did the drama sustain the students' interest?

❏ Did the group as a whole enjoy the drama? Did individuals within the group enjoy it?

❏ Did the drama stimulate production of artwork and written material?

❏ Was the relationship between teacher and students reasonably relaxed? stiff and uneasy? too informal for control to be maintained?

❏ How appealing and/or challenging did the students appear to find the work?

❏ If music, props, costumes, masks, special effects, and the like were used, did they enhance the drama?

❏ Were the students aware of communicating to others, developing a sense of audience?

❏ What might follow in subsequent drama lessons?

_____

_____

_____

_____

_____

Planning for Future Drama Activities

To help plan further activities appropriate to students' developing abilities, you might find it useful to ask yourself these questions about the work already completed.

- ❏ What kinds of activities did I set up for the class and how did I set them up?

- ❏ What kinds of questions and statements did I use?

- ❏ Were my intentions presented clearly to the class, or was there some confusion in my thinking?

- ❏ How did I function in the class? Did I take a role, inquire, insist, monitor, direct?

- ❏ How was the lesson divided? Were students talking, reflecting, testing ideas, exploring, arguing, negotiating, challenging, and researching?

- ❏ Did the strategies I used help me meet my intention?

- ❏ Did I change direction during the lesson? If so, why?

- ❏ What was the effect of my changing direction?

- ❏ Did the pace of the dramatic action allow the class time to build belief in the situation?

- ❏ Which activities did the class initiate?

- ❏ Did the class give me signals that I could read in order to change the direction of the lesson?

- ❏ Did the attitude of the class change for better or worse during the lesson? What did I have to do with these changes?

- ❏ What things was I driven by in the lesson: time, pace, interruptions by the students?

- ❏ Did changes occur in class groupings? How and why did these changes occur?

- ❏ What kinds of learning occurred in the lesson?

- ❏ What learning areas were established for exploration in future lessons?

- ❏ What reflection time was encouraged?

- ❏ Did I allow time for self-assessment?

_____

_____

_____

_____

_____

A Checklist for Assessing Growth in and through the Arts in Education

Arts-Making: Expressing and Communicating Ideas and Feelings through the Arts Forms

- ❏ Accepts the teacher as an arts instructor and an arts maker
- ❏ Demonstrates a willingness to discover, experiment with, and explore different arts forms and materials
- ❏ Selects, shapes and presents ideas and feelings through a variety of arts forms and materials
- ❏ Expresses inventive and innovative ideas through an arts form
- ❏ Finds satisfaction in making and creating artistic products and events
- ❏ Is emotionally and intellectually engaged in the arts work
- ❏ Is willing to revise, shape and work towards improving and completing the arts work
- ❏ Expresses ideas and feelings freely and without fear of judgment
- ❏ Is willing to take risks when working independently or with others
- ❏ Sustains involvement from initiating, following through, to completing arts work
- ❏ Applies a developing knowledge of the elements of the arts form
- ❏ Applies prior learning (skills, concepts, techniques) and draws on personal background in the development of the arts form
- ❏ Demonstrates continuing growth in the ability to communicate ideas and feelings through arts forms
- ❏ Incorporates a variety of multimedia and technology in arts learning
- ❏ Transfers knowledge of the ideas explored in curriculum areas into personal arts work
- ❏ Transforms ideas represented in one arts form into another composition using a different arts form
- ❏ Uses metaphor, symbolism and abstraction in arts making
- ❏ Demonstrates an understanding of the basic elements of the different arts forms
- ❏ Discriminates and makes effective choices for specific artistic purposes
- ❏ Elaborates ideas in arts works by adding, omitting, distorting, and/or exaggerating
- ❏ Experiences the arts of different cultures
- ❏ Uses tools, equipment, materials appropriately and effectively

- ❏ Explores a variety of sources for ideas for arts making

- ❏ Investigates a variety of possibilities for using different arts forms

- ❏ Researches information for artistic compositions

- ❏ Seeks possibilities, finds alternatives and explores ideas in-depth through the arts

- ❏ Accepts and supports the contributions of others in creating an ensemble arts work

- ❏ Creates arts events as a member of an ensemble

- ❏ Develops and shares ideas and materials

- ❏ Is able to discuss the process involved in producing the arts work

- ❏ Is aware of audience, adopting appropriate style and content

- ❏ Is receptive to advice from others

- ❏ Presents arts work publicly

Arts Literacy: Demonstrating Awareness and Knowledge about the Arts Forms

- ❏ Appreciates and interprets the arts work of peers and professionals

- ❏ Appreciates different ideas, styles and products

- ❏ Appreciates the effects of form on the meaning of what is seen and heard

- ❏ Defines the elements and principles of the arts form, and uses them when responding to arts works

- ❏ Describes how artists representing various periods, styles, and cultures have used materials, tools, elements and the principles of the arts form for a variety of purposes

- ❏ Identifies and describes types and genres of arts events

- ❏ Identifies factors that affect our understanding of the arts

- ❏ Identifies ideas evoked by the artist or the work

- ❏ Recognizes the implications of commercial arts forms

- ❏ Sees similarities and differences in a wide range of artistic styles in each arts form

- ❏ Understands how the ideas in arts works relate to their own knowledge and experience

- ❏ Demonstrates appropriate viewing and listening behaviors in response to an arts work or event

- ❏ Appreciates displays and installations in school

- ❏ Participates in arts events with guests and during excursions

- ❏ Communicates understanding and knowledge of the arts form in appropriate ways

- ❏ Demonstrates knowledge of aspects of the historical context of an arts product or event
- ❏ Describes products, performances and events, and distinguishes between the types or styles used
- ❏ Differentiates between stereotypes and truthful interpretations in arts products and events
- ❏ Makes and understands artistic and aesthetic choices
- ❏ Recognizes the value of arts experiences, both as maker and viewer, and as interpreter and critic
- ❏ Uses the terminology of the arts form
- ❏ Reflects upon and assesses own work orally and in writing
- ❏ Demonstrates a growing understanding of overall effect of arts forms (elements, principles, techniques, styles)
- ❏ Has an awareness of unity and coherence in the arts forms
- ❏ Explains key ideas, concepts and personal connections that emerge in the arts work
- ❏ Explains a preference for specific arts works
- ❏ Reflects on personal learning and growth in an arts form
- ❏ Shares connections, ideas and insights with others
- ❏ Applies artistic and aesthetic learning to other areas and aspects of life
- ❏ Demonstrates empathy and consideration for the work of others
- ❏ Keeps an arts portfolio of arts products, reflections, and resources
- ❏ Examines ideology and values presented in the arts forms
- ❏ Listens, reflects on, and thinks critically about the arts works of others
- ❏ Gives personal and informed opinions about an arts event
- ❏ Responds affectively and cognitively to arts works and events

_____

_____

_____

_____

_____

_____

Index